This book is a perceptive analysis using four biblical passages of the hidden agendas that can lurk in each human heart. With appropriate and often deeply moving pastoral insights from his own life and refreshing honesty, the author reveals these agendas and the corresponding heart problems they generate. He shows us how to deal with them in such a way as to banish a series of our common fears:

1. Our fear of insignificance by building godly character into our lives rather than a tower of self-aggrandisement;

2. Our fear of the dark and uncertainty by seeking God's light and guidance and learning to trust Him, rather than idolatrously relying on our own powers of understanding and illumination;

3. Our fear of living outside the flimsy whitewashed walls of our comfort zones and daring to trust God and rest in the security of His peace in the face of storm, danger and threat that calls for courage and sacrifice;

4. Our fear that God cannot satisfy our thirst for fulfilment so that we rely on our own inadequate resources to dig our own store cisterns where there is no water rather than turning to God who He is able constantly to supply living water to refresh us.

I thoroughly recommend it as a book to strengthen our confidence in the adequacy of God.

JOHN LENNOX
Emeritus Professor of Mathematics, University of Oxford
Author of several books, including *Where is God in a Coronavirus World?*

T0016765

This is an important book which explores an area which most of us prefer to ignore, the difficult subject of the inner motives that drive us. As followers of Jesus Christ we may plan, strategize, and set out goals—all worthy activities, but the difficult task of searching our hearts, or even more challenging, of allowing God to do this, is easily neglected. Through pertinent biblical examples, David Smith helps us to dig deeper into our heart motives. He examines the stories of those who chose to make a name for themselves, or walked by their own light, covered up decay to maintain peace and harmony, or placed personal fulfilment above the service and glory of God. These are challenging chapters, especially when compared with the highest model of service, for we are called to follow our Lord who washed the feet of others. A highly recommended read for all.

IAN BURNESS
Chairman, IBCM Network

Like an annual physical exam, it is good to get a spiritual heart check now and again. *Hidden Agendas* does that by helping us see things that get in the way of our walk with God and then prescribing ways to renew our heart trust in God. The result is a healthier walk with God. So read and grow.

DARRELL BOCK
Executive Director for Cultural Engagement, Howard G. Hendricks
Center for Christian Leadership and Cultural Engagement
Senior Research Professor of New Testament Studies,
Dallas Theological Seminary, Dallas, Texas

We live in a generation in which it is unpopular to talk about sins of the heart. That is why this book is important. Smith is like a spiritual surgeon who tests and scans for hidden motivations, then skillfully and lovingly cuts them out. As I read, I found myself entreating the Lord through the sentiments of Psalm 139 to search and know my heart, test and know my thoughts, uncover hidden agendas, and lead me in His ways.

KENNETH BERDING
Professor of New Testament, Talbot School of Theology,
Biola University, Los Angeles, California
Author of *How To Live An 'In Christ' Life: 100 Devotional Readings on Union with Christ*

Hidden Agendas by David Smith is a helpful and refreshing book. David writes with the mind of a scholar but the heart of an experienced pastor to search deep into the human heart and identify weaknesses that we all have and need to deal with. In each chapter he draws examples of weaknesses and 'hidden agendas' from scripture and then uses scripture to provide the answers. Each chapter then ends with a helpful summary and some reflective questions. This book would be a help to anyone in ministry or leadership, however experienced or inexperienced. It provides a vital health check and should be a must read for practitioners.

STEPHEN MCQUOID
Director of GLO-Europe

To my family,
with whom I share the pilgrimage of life –
Judy, Daniel, Danielle, Aidan, Jessica, Kaila.

DAVID A. SMITH

HIDDEN AGENDAS

Demands of the heart that stop us loving God and others

CHRISTIAN
FOCUS

Copyright © David A. Smith 2022

paperback ISBN 978-1-5271-0836-3
ebook ISBN 978-1-5271-0904-9

10 9 8 7 6 5 4 3 2 1

Published in 2022
by
Christian Focus Publications, Ltd.
Geanies House, Fearn,
Ross-shire, IV20 1TW, Scotland.
www.christianfocus.com

Cover design by Rubner Durais

Printed and bound by
Bell & Bain, Glasgow

CONTENTS

Agendas

1

Agendas

This book lifts the lid on the human heart, seeking to uncover the hidden agendas that stop us from loving God and others as we should.

What is an agenda? We most commonly use the word 'agenda' in the context of a meeting where we discuss ideas and make decisions. The agenda is circulated prior to the meeting and contains the important issues that need to be attended to. The other meaning of agenda is connected but more goal directed. We say, 'My agenda is to achieve a desired outcome.' Of which we may have many. Our heart agendas are similar and combine both meanings. Our heart agendas are the list of priorities that we believe are important and need to be given attention, so we achieve our desired outcomes. However, the agenda of a board meeting is always made public, whereas the agendas of our heart are often hidden, certainly from others, and often even from ourselves. We seldom stop and listen to our heart and are therefore mostly ignorant of the agendas of our heart. So, perhaps unintentionally and unknowingly, we serve the hidden agendas and desired outcomes of our own heart rather than serving God and others to the full. This is akin to when Paul says,

> For I do not do the good I want to do, but the evil I do not want to do—this I keep on doing.[1]

Paul has listened to his heart and he knows that his own agenda and God's agenda are often in tension. Do we even realize there is an agenda struggle in our heart? If we are serious about serving God's agenda rather than our own heart agenda, we need to uncover these hidden agenda items so that we can serve God and others rather than ourselves.

Using four biblical pictures we pause to take time and consider our hidden heart agendas. We explore their underlying fears to identify their demands and problems and to make us aware of how God wants to apprehend, awaken, shape and transform our hearts. Through these pictures we consider four major underlying heart agendas that often remain undetected in our lives.

I am convinced that many of us are blind to these agendas and some never wake up from the slumber of ignorance when it comes to the desires of the heart. We talk about idolatry in terms of what we worship. Things like wealth, reputation, career, sex and status. But we never wake up and grasp what is feeding the self-idolatry that makes these things so attractive.

---

1   Romans 7:19

We spend time analysing and planning the best ways to do life and ministry, coming up with confident options and strategies, not aware of how our hidden and mostly selfish longings may be directing our thoughts and decisions along the way. We care for all those around us, even loving them and desiring the best for them, oblivious to the fact that God's best for them and us may collide with our own ideas. We seek the abundant life of which Jesus speaks, all the time confusing it for our hunger for the good life. So we strive for the good life when God's agenda for us is the best life, not our little heaven on earth bubble that we create for ourselves here and now.

As you read further some may ask why I didn't include a chapter on our longing for love in the book. Because you would say, 'We all need and long for love.' Surely it must be one of our agendas. And you would be correct. However, firstly the agenda of love is not so hidden, and secondly, if you look closely you will find that our search or demand for love follows various paths. Once you have read the book, I believe that you will agree with me that love seeks approval in the eyes of others, love seeks clarity through the agreement of others, love seeks protection in the arms of others, and love seeks abundance in life with others. It is these more particular and hidden paths that we consider in this book.

Some may also wonder where the Holy Spirit has gone from this book. Surely, you say, everything is not as bad as you portray; you have forgotten that the Holy Spirit is constantly seeking to focus our eyes away from self and our hidden agendas, whatever they may be, and onto Christ, so that we follow His call and not the call of our hearts. Of course we desire to seek God, and His will, and long to be like Christ. But just like Paul describes, our human heart left unchecked, drives us in other directions.

I want us to focus on the hidden drift of our heart that often goes unnoticed in the busyness and noise of the cycle of life. The Holy Spirit will be right there with us as we take this journey.

Like Paul, we are clearly in this wrestle of the flesh and the Spirit. We have the desire to do what is good, but we struggle to carry it out.[2] Yes, we desire to serve God. Yes, we desire to love God and others. Why is it that we so often fall so short? Here, we uncover the problem. Through lifting the lid on our hidden heart agendas we discover that if they are left unidentified and unchecked, they will choke our relationships with God and others and suffocate our ministry and service for Him.

As you read I ask you to also feel the words. Do not read just with your mind, trying to take in the information, checking to see if it is correct and valuable and should be added to your treasury of spiritual knowledge. But read with your heart. Be open to feeling the Spirit impress upon you the times and places where you identify with what is being said.

I pray that you feel the Spirit awaken you to a new awareness of your heart's agendas. I pray that you feel the fear of your heart and understand how you have learned to respond, sometimes in ways that have taken you away from God and others. I pray that you feel the demands that you put on God and others, and how these can hinder you from fully loving, serving, trusting and valuing firstly God and then others also. But most of all I pray that you will feel the heart of God for you. That you understand the full significance of being His child, that He holds you in His hands, and that His heart is set on all that is abundantly good for you. He wants your heart to be in tune with His heart.

---

2   Romans 7:18

In the concluding chapter I refer to an illustration of a ship tied up at a wharf with the ropes of our hidden agendas. Now it's time to take a look at each of these, to identify our hidden agendas, and commence the releasing of those ropes to embark on a true heart pilgrimage.

City Builders

2

City Builders

The Story

The people of that ancient time only existed because of the grace of God in saving Noah and his family, eight in all. The deliverance from the flood by God was now a distant memory. The descendants of Noah were no longer a single clan, their numbers were swelling, and people were dispersing across the land. Some moved eastward, coming down from the hill country, settling on a plain in Shinar, in Babylonia, in search of something more. We all want something more!

Urban planning became the topic of conversation. Rather than roaming as tribal nomads, as in the past, they wanted to settle, to put down roots, to establish themselves, and to make a city. And not just any city – a grand city, with an enormous tower (ziggurat), bigger than anything else around. Who doesn't like big? So, they began to build on the banks of the mighty Euphrates River. Genesis 11:1–9 reads:

Now the whole world had one language and a common speech. As people moved eastward, they found a plain in Shinar and settled there. They said to each other, 'Come, let's make bricks and bake them thoroughly.' They used brick instead of stone, and tar for mortar. Then they said, 'Come, let us build ourselves a city, with a tower that reaches to the heavens, so that we may make a name for ourselves; otherwise we will be scattered over the face of the whole earth.' But the Lord came down to see the city and the tower the people were building. The Lord said, 'If as one people speaking the same language they have begun to do this, then nothing they plan to do will be impossible for them. Come, let us go down and confuse their language so they will not understand each other.' So the Lord scattered them from there over all the earth, and they stopped building the city. That is why it was called Babel— because there the Lord confused the language of the whole world. From there the Lord scattered them over the face of the whole earth.

Why the desire for more and big? What was stirring in the hearts of the people at this time? What made them say, 'Come let us build ourselves a city with a tower that reaches to the heavens'? Was there enough of a memory of the flood that they were fearful of another being sent their way by God? Perhaps, but this would also mean that they had completely forgotten the covenant that God had made with Noah, saying that He would never destroy the earth by flood again.[1] Or had they completely forgotten God, and they were now pursuing other gods? Most likely.

Part of ancient pagan worship included building a high tower, known as a religious ziggurat, to reach the heavens, the

---

1   Genesis 9:11

home of the gods. Religion was the centre of life and the ziggurat was the centre of the city. The religious tower had a square base with a stairway rising up and around each side, ascending to the summit, upon which a temple was built. The temple on the tower top was the heavenly or godly place, where sacrifices would be offered and where gods would come down and meet with the people. It was their heaven on earth, their gateway to the gods; it was Babel.[2]

Now these people didn't want any old tower. Whatever other function it served, it is recorded that they wanted to commence the enormous building project 'so that we may make a name for ourselves; otherwise we will be scattered over the face of the whole earth.' With God long forgotten, or at most a faint fear factor, the people had lost any alternative basis for establishing their identity. As nomads at risk of becoming nobodies, being scattered and lost across the face of the earth as disparate tribes, their hearts turned to filling their need of a sense of identity, by creating a reputation.

In ancient times greatness was measured in terms of numbers of people in your tribe, the size of the flocks and herds of animals in your possession, the enormity of structures built, and the height and thickness of city walls. To be a people of substance, of known value and identity, you would have a powerful god who visits you, and you would have all the necessary appearances of being a powerful people. Having the largest tower with the highest temple would go a long way to ensuring you attract the most powerful god and become the most significant people on earth. They didn't want to be lost to the footnotes of history;

2   Babel sounds like the Hebrew word for 'confused'. The name Babel in its Assyrian form, *Bābilī*, means 'gate of god'. Bromiley, *The International Standard Bible Encyclopedia*, (V1):382.

they wanted something more, to be known far and wide. They wanted to make a name for themselves. A big name.

Heart Agenda

Their heart agenda was to be significant. They desired a great name and they thought a giant tower was the key to success.

It's no different today. Big towers that reach to the heavens: the tower of Babel (Babylonia), the great pyramids (Egypt), the Eiffel Tower (France), the Empire State Building (USA), the Petronas Towers (Malaysia), the Taipei Tower (Taiwan), the Shanghai Tower (China), the Burj Khalifa (UAE), and more under construction. The planners are still planning. The builders are still building. The presidents still want to make their nations great!

Where is the end? Are the planners, the builders, and the countries all trying to make a name for themselves? Are they seeking an identity, a reputation? Are they wanting to be considered significant? Probably! What is certain is that they don't want the opposite to be true. They don't want to be left behind, forgotten, insignificant. Just like the people of ancient times, being insignificant nobodies is not on their agenda. And so, with a heart bent on significance, with all the energy they have, the people of Babylonia commence construction. Having no stone or mortar they begin making a name for themselves out of bricks and tar.

What about you? It's not just the people of Babel, or the large cities of this world that have this heart desire, this heart agenda. You and I do too. Our heart's agenda is to be significant. We all want to be a somebody, to make a name for ourselves. And so we become city builders just like the people of Babel.

How do we build? It happens every day, through symbols, achievements, associations, and our words. Left unguarded our heart is constantly pulsating, to move us onward and upward, to make our name bigger and better, becoming more significant.

Our world is full of symbols. We are constantly pressured to believe that identifying with certain symbols will somehow impart significance upon us, elevating us to new heights through association. Symbols stand for something beyond the object itself. They are markers of a greater meaning. You don't just buy a pair of running shoes. You buy 'Nike' shoes. And by acquiring the 'Nike' symbol, you not only get footwear, but you feel like you receive the ability to immediately associate yourself with the images of all the sporting heroes that contribute to the meaning and significance of the name. You are elevated in status, becoming significant by wearing a name. Just do it, 'Nike', and you will become more we are told. And so we accumulate symbols as markers of success and significance, like trophies to our own great name. Labels on clothes, cars and clubs, horses and handbags, houses and holiday destinations, watches and wine, suburbs, shoes, shirts and schools. These along with smartphones, laptops and devices of all types serve beyond their function to build our identity, our significance. And the more symbols we can accumulate the better.

We build our name through achievements. From a young age we learn that we are affirmed when we perform well and achieve much, and when we don't, we are ignored or even criticized. Our early years provide us with a myriad of opportunities to sort out where we shine and where we don't. When we don't shine, we tend to file that information away and say to ourselves 'Well, we won't try that again will we.' But when we do receive affirmation and applause and feel like we have achieved something, we pursue it. If it's sports, we strive harder, if it's looks, we beautify, if it's academics, we immerse ourselves, if it's our career we climb the ladder, if it's humour, we become the best clown around. All in an effort to achieve that illusive significance, while all the time avoiding situations where we might look foolish or fail. We want that high feeling of success, not that low feeling of inadequacy. So we chase it. More achievements. Regular achievements. Larger achievements. Like a drug, clamouring after as much as we can get to build up our name.

We build our name through associations, who we are connected to, and what we are part of. Our associations matter to us. We want to be in not out. We want to be accepted not rejected. We want to be associated with the somebodies, not excluded and abandoned, a nobody. My friends, my family, my school, my city, my country, my football team. Even though I don't play in the football team, and even though I don't own the football team, I still say it's 'my' team. When they win, I say it loud and often! When they are not doing so well, I keep quiet; I then only mention my allegiance if pushed, as if their poor performance is attacking my net worth.

The people around us form a special means of gaining significance by association. We name drop. Why? We want to be seen as associating with winners, those of significant or popular standing. Sporting heroes, celebrities, movie stars, community leaders, knowledgeable professionals, rulers – actually anyone who will impress others. Then I can ride on their coat-tails and feel as though I am elevated in some way. Deep down we hope that by being connected with significant others their status will rub off onto us. Of course, we know this doesn't literally happen, but we love the feeling of hoping somehow it will. Or we pray that something else magical will take place. That the minds of others will be changed. That because of my association with another they will, all of a sudden, view me from a completely different and elevated point of view. I want association status to rub off onto me, and I want others to believe it. Have you ever tried using something as tangential as 'You'll never guess who I saw at the airport the other day'? What are we doing? Passing on information? Yes. But also secretly hoping that we move up one notch in the significance stakes, especially if we casually drop it into conversation at the right time.

The words we say and the conversations we hold can actually become battles for significance. Conversations, while vehicles for information exchange, are mechanisms we can use to impress others, hoping to gain significance points. We often play the one-up game. Why? We want to make a name for ourselves, pure and simple. You are in a group with friends and someone starts a conversation about the size of the fish that they caught over the weekend. Then another person chimes in with a story about the enormous catch they made last summer on vacation. And on and on it goes with the fish and the stories getting larger and more colourful. So what do you do? Join in and tell the story about your biggest catch. But maybe you don't fish, and you certainly don't have a story about catching a shark or a whale. But you play golf and so to join in the one-up game, you tell a colourful story about the hole in one you scored recently. Or someone tells a joke, which is followed by another which is even funnier, then a third and a fourth, growing in hilarity each time. Each joke is in some small way a search, not just for laughs but for significance. Then the conversation changes completely. Someone is criticized. And before long everyone is on the band wagon, criticizing the person. Everyone may feel it is justified. But that's not all they feel. They feel good about themselves for a moment. Why? Because putting another down elevates yourself. That's why criticism and gossip are rampant. Who doesn't want to feel better about themselves? Who doesn't want to feel more important?

More recently social media has given the city builders another tool with which to build their significance tower. The right text, the right look, the right photo, the right comment, that witty meme, all agonized over to achieve greatest effect, and targeted to serve the desire for more. We want to be liked, actually and digitally. In the eyes of others we want to be viewed as significant. And if we are honest, not only do we want to be considered significant, but we want to be more significant than others. Because it's only then that we can be satisfied with ourselves that we are not a failure, a nobody. Or in such situations do you remain silent, having no story, no joke, no post, feeling invisible, again?

Heart Fear

That is our greatest fear, being invisible, being thought of as nothing, insignificant, a failure. What did the people of Babel fear? Being insignificant, being less than others. And so we also strive in our own strength to build something significant out of our lives.

There is an insidious sin at work in the significance factory of our lives driven by the fear of failure. It is the sin of comparison. There would be no gauge for success and therefore significance without comparison. We only know we are significant when we can measure the size of our city tower and compare it to others. When we can compare aspects of our lives with others and determine that our name is indeed great, only then are we satisfied. Comparison is a measuring stick designed to effectively serve self-centredness rather than other-centredness. The disciples suffered from this.

Jesus had taken the disciples to a private place to talk to them about His upcoming suffering, death and resurrection. But the disciples did not really grasp what He was saying. They were preoccupied with thinking that Jesus would be victorious and not suffer, would build a new kingdom and not be buried, and would reign as king, without the need for resurrection. They were arguing between themselves over who would get the prime positions in their imaginary kingdom with Jesus. Their hearts were on a search for greater significance. They were busy comparing each other's merits, trying to ascertain how they could ensure that they would get the priority seats. So Jesus confronts them at the end of their journey as they come to Capernaum. 'What were you arguing about on the road?'[3] Jesus says. No answer. Embarrassment. They knew it was wrong to argue about who was to be the greatest – especially with the King. Perhaps this was the first time someone had confronted them and lifted the lid on their significance agenda, their self-idolatry.

Embarrassment must have turned to confusion with the betrayal of Jesus by Judas in the garden. The kingdom where they had hoped to take important seats was now being threatened. So Peter, fearing it would all be taken away, drew his sword as if he would take on the entire detachment of advancing soldiers. He managed to take an ear, but they took Jesus away. His hope was arrested. Things were deteriorating quickly. He followed Jesus as far as the High Priest's courtyard but had to wait outside. In the cool night air Peter stood around the open fire warming

---

3   Mark 9:30-34

himself with other bystanders to the main action. Now what? Continue to follow Jesus or start to seek something else? The outcome of this kingdom didn't look so grand any more. He was brought back from his thoughts with a start by a servant girl who asked, 'You aren't one of this man's disciples too, are you?' Peter, outside, in the cold, found himself scrambling to protect what remained of his diminishing significance. Maybe he thought, 'If I admit I'm with Jesus it looks like it's all downhill from here. But if I deny it then I may have a chance at least of reclaiming my former life back.' So he said to the servant girl across the flickering flames and through the swirling smoke, 'I am not.'[4] He denies his connection to Jesus twice more when questioned by others standing outside around the fire. The cock crows, Jesus looks, and Peter goes outside and weeps bitterly.[5] All his significance is lost, he is a complete failure. In the eyes of Jesus, in the eyes of the servants, in his own eyes, his worst nightmare had just occurred. He was afraid of failure, of being a nothing. He thought it was all coming together with Jesus and His kingdom. But now what he had built up in his own mind was all crashing down around him.

The next time we see Peter he is in Galilee and has gone fishing with his friends. He knows fishing; it is familiar and he is good at it. At least out on the lake he feels like someone, not great perhaps, but someone doing something that others in the community around Capernaum will appreciate. Some significance again; well, not a failure at least. Does Peter love Jesus above himself and his friends? Has he put himself first and following Jesus second? The next time that Jesus and Peter

---

4   John 18:15-18

5   Luke 22:60-62

meet, along the shores of Galilee after an unsuccessful night of fishing, Jesus asks him this exact question. 'Peter, do you love me?'[6]

Perhaps this is the first time you have thought about your own self-idolatry in these terms. You desire significance, you fear failure, and you go to whatever lengths are required to feel better, to be more. Your heart agenda is to idolize self. You demand significance, and you run from failure.

Heart Demand

When we follow our heart agenda of significance and allow our fear of failure to take over, our heart becomes demanding. It demands others make us look good. It demands others affirm our worth. It demands others accept us.

Let's take a closer look at what we do. When you are with a group of people what do you want from them? You at least want to be accepted as normal. That's fine. But ask yourself how many times are you concerned, silently inside, about how others are perceiving you? Be honest! Often, we are hoping that we don't make a fool of ourselves. Are we dressed OK? Do we look awkward? Don't stumble! Don't say something out of place! Oh the pressure of being accepted! We just want someone to agree with us, to laugh at our jokes, to say something good about us, to tell us that we are OK. We want others to come through for us and make us look good. We are constantly in a social battle, requiring others to affirm our worth. How selfish, how idolatrous!

As a Bible College lecturer I frequently run classes on preaching. One of the first things I tell students is that if you want

---

6   John 21

to learn how to preach effectively you must learn how to get over yourself. In other words you must learn how to not think about what others are thinking about you. Your mind must only focus on communicating the message clearly to others. Don't think about whether you look good. Don't think about whether the hearers accept you. Don't desire to have them affirm your worth. You are there to serve them only, not your own ego or image. If you think about what others are thinking about you, you will become self-serving and inward looking, rather than serving others and outward focused. This is often not only the first but also the hardest lesson for preachers to learn.

As a preacher myself, I am not immune to this issue, not generally during the delivery of the message, but after the sermon. I conclude and say the final prayer and then step away from the pulpit and out to the congregation. The people at this time are just starting to move, striking up their first conversations, or going out for coffee. What do I want? Coffee? Of course! But more than that I have a restlessness inside that I want to get rid of. It is a question. And it is about me. How did I do? I want someone to come up to me and tell me that my preaching was good, or better still brilliant, so that I can feel significant again. Being aware of it I try and suppress it, but it creeps out.

But wait there's more. As I write this, we are in the midst of the coronavirus lockdown. No church gatherings allowed. We adapted and have begun to livestream our services into the homes of our members and others who wish to join us. I finish preaching and there is no one other than the technicians to come and tell me that I did OK. But who needs that when now there's on-screen feedback all the time? I know at any moment how many people are watching live and how many people have clicked on the link and viewed the sermon after. Unless it's my father watching me over and over. Thanks Dad. Our digital world is now designed to feed our significance at the click of a mouse on the screen, instantly.

It's so easy to treat relationships the same way, as the click of our 'like' icon. When we fall in love, we give ourselves a big significance tick! We feel loved and we feel significant at the same time. How good is that? But, do we fall in love with serving and valuing the other above all else? That is our call. Or do we fall in love with the other because they value us and thus feed our heart's desire?

This is where my wife and I start our conversation in the first session of pre-marriage counselling. We sit the couple down and after only a few minutes I ask, 'So are you both ready to give your life to each other?' to which they normally say 'Yes, of course. We love each other and we want to be together for life. That is why we are here.' I say, 'That is not what I mean. I mean are your both ready to die for each other, to give your whole lives away to each other, because that's what marriage is all about?' Silence.

When our heart strongly demands significance from others, relationships become something we can easily use to build our towers of significance rather than opportunities to express the self-giving love of God. And when they don't serve to build us up, we reject them and try someone else. Build me up or I will let you down becomes our mode of relational operation. Then we get married, and with our voice vow in all circumstances to sacrifice everything, all the while hoping that the one we make the promise to will be a lifelong guaranteed source of significance. So while we promise sacrifice, we demand significance till death do us part. We need to ensure our relational heart and vows do not look something like this:

> I need to feel important and I expect you to meet that need by submitting to my every decision, whether good or bad; by respecting me no matter how I behave; and by supporting me in whatever I choose to do. I want you to treat me as the most important [person] in the world. My goal in marrying you is to find my significance through you.[7]

What are you thinking about when you enter relationships, or even enter church for that matter? Will I be accepted and valued? What will I get out of this? Do I look OK? What are others thinking? I hope my children don't play up! Where are my friends that like me and will make me feel good? Or is our focus where it should be, on others and on God? We so easily get sucked into feeding this heart demand for significance. It is a heart problem.

Heart Problem

So did I preach for God or for my own sense of significance? You may say, 'Well everyone does it, so what is the big deal?' It's true that everyone chases more and more significance for themselves. The problem is that it is just like stealing.

It's like the story of Achan in the book of Joshua.[8] The Israelites had recently crossed the River Jordan and entered the Promised Land with only what they carried. All equal. They created a pile of twelve stones, one for each tribe, as a reminder of the provision and faithfulness of God. Then they had together just experienced the power of God in the fall of

---

7   Crabb, *The Marriage Builder*, 31.

8   Joshua 7

Jericho. They were all provided for by God. But Achan wanted more. During the battle of Ai he stole articles that were to be devoted to the glory of God. But he wanted more for himself, which always means less for others, and in this case less for God. Achan wanted to make himself more significant, more valuable, by taking that which was valuable away from others and God.

When we want more for ourselves, when we want to be seen as more significant, more valuable, we actually take value away from others. When we desire more, we are actually saying to others 'Look at me!' And when we do this, we are not able to look at others and value them as we should. Those around us are reduced to pawns in our game of self-aggrandizement. Driven on by our constant fear of failure, we use others, their comments, their affirmations and their acceptance, as fuel to feed our insatiable desire for significance. As if that's not bad enough, we then find ourselves also stealing glory from God by doubting Him.

When we are busy building our own significance, we are at the same time doubting our own value. And when we are doubting our own value, we are doubting whether God really values us. We show we doubt God and reduce His glory in two ways. We turn God into a blessing machine. This is where our faith in God is conditional upon God continually blessing us with increased signs of significance, in life through symbols, in relationships through affirmation, and in ministry through success. Or if this fails, we turn our back on God and start building our own towers of importance in our own way. We use relationships to feed our own egos rather than really caring for people. We use ministry to create moments and crowds that will adore and worship our gifts and abilities as much as worship God. We live life on our own terms, striving our utmost in our own strength to achieve our own sense of significance, in whatever way we can, no matter how fleeting. All the while we believe that God is not enough for us, He is too small for us.

When we use others and God to feed our own value, we cannot, at the same time, value others and God as we should. When we are at this point, whether we realize it or not, we should not be surprised if God moves to wake us up from our heart problem, much like a defibrillator jolt, bringing us back to life.

At another time, in a similar place, a king arose from the descendants of the original city builders. His name was Nebuchadnezzar. He too was a significant city builder. One of his most famous constructions was that of the golden statue, bearing the image of either a god or himself as king. The image of gold was 27 metres high and 2.7 metres wide. Not satisfied with the grandeur of the statue alone, Nebuchadnezzar proceeded to command all to fall down and worship the image of gold.[9] He wanted more than power, which he already had, and that more than most. Through the image, Nebuchadnezzar wanted to join the power he already held over his kingdom with the religious act of worship. He wanted people to now worship his power, in essence to worship him. His heart agenda was the same as his ancestors. He desired significance through power and worship and would stop at nothing to get it. Yet the great Nebuchadnezzar would soon be humbled by God, judged and put out to pasture to eat grass like an ox.[10] As he walked on the roof of his royal palace, surveying all he had done he said:

---

9   Daniel 3

10   Daniel 4

Is not this the great Babylon I have built as the royal residence,
by my mighty power and for the glory of my majesty?[11]

As soon as he said this, God took away his significance and glory,
and he became like an ox for seven years until he acknowledged

that the Most High is sovereign over all kingdoms on earth
and gives them to anyone he wishes.[12]

This is not the last we hear of Babylon in the Bible. Babylon
is constantly referred to as the place that sets itself up as being
against God, or anti-God. The final reference to Babylon is in
the book of Revelation[13] where we see the city, one of the greatest
cities, pictured as going up in smoke, destroyed by the sovereign
God. For Babel and Babylon, chasing a name, pursuing the
heart agenda of significance in the place of acknowledging God,
ended in confusion, judgement and destruction.

As the sun sets on the story in the plain of Shinar, the one
true God came down to visit the people gathered at Babel. With
His hands He opened the heavens and descended to see what
the people were doing. With their hearts turned against Him
and set on building towers to honour other gods, including
self-idolization, He confused their languages, and scattered the
people across the world, humbling them, taking away their self-
made significance, wanting them to find themselves and their
significance in Him alone.

---

11   Daniel 4:30
12   Daniel 4:32
13   Revelation 18–19:3

God's Heart Agenda

God's agenda for our heart all starts with our image, not our impression or self-made images of ourselves but the fact that we are created in the very image of God.[14] This means two things. Firstly, that our significance is connected to God. And secondly that we are all created equal.

If we are created in the image of God, then our source of significance can only come from our creator. It's just like in the *Toy Story* movies. Woody the toy cowboy is worried that others will take his place as Andy's favourite toy. He finds his significance in the eyes of his owner, and the opinion of the other toys is far less important.

It should be the same for us. We are intimately created and infinitely valued children of God.[15] We must find our significance, which indeed we need, in one place only – the eyes of God. We must not look for it in the eyes of others, or from the building of our own towers and cities, designed to attract attention to ourselves and away from others and God.

Being made in the image of God also means that we are created equal – equal in value. We are equal in value no matter what our eyes see, no matter what the world says and no matter what value system is used in our own countries, because we are citizens of a better country that is not from here.[16] Therefore, it only matters what God sees, and what God says.

The Corinthians had a problem with significance. They were all puffed-up with their own importance. Some looked down on the others, parading their gifts around as if certain

---

14   Genesis 1:26-27

15   Psalm 8, Psalm 139:13-16, John 3:16

16   Philippians 3:20

ones made them more spiritual and important in the eyes of God and others. They were taking what God had given them, the gifts, and turning them into something about themselves. They took what came from God and pretended that it was of their own doing.

We tend to do the same. We take what God has given us, our own life, our gifts, our abilities, and then we go off on our own to make a name for ourselves out of the very things God has gifted to us. We act as if we have successfully created our own significance by ourselves. As if out of nothing we have built our own lives. However, only God creates from nothing. We can take what He gives to us and use it, either to bring glory to His name, or to make a name for ourselves.

So Paul tells the Corinthians that they have it all wrong. The gifts speak of God's goodness not of their significance. He says:

> But God has put the body together, giving greater honour to the parts that lacked it, so that there should be no division in the body, but that its parts should have equal concern for each other.[17]

Every part has the same honour because the hand of God makes every part. We are all unique, yet all have the same value. Each one of us does not have all the gifts. Therefore, we are each dependent on others to be our hands and feet, to fill in the gaps that we leave open. That means we need each other. It should orient us toward humility and away from the arrogance of overinflated significance. On the other hand we are all gifted, which means we each have equal significance, but this comes from the giver not the gifts. The value that our Father the King

---

17   1 Corinthians 12:24-25

of heaven places upon each one of us, His children, should be our only concern.

We can so easily be tempted to make a name for ourselves, to look down on others, like the people of Babel, or the Corinthians. This takes us back to the story of Jesus with the disciples who were still fighting for first place. What does Jesus do? He takes a child in His arms and says:

> Anyone who wants to be first must be the very last, and the servant of all.[18]

He turns the world upside down. Significance, status, power and place are not part of my kingdom, He says. If you want to be part of my work and world, it means acting with humility, service and faithful reliance, being totally dependent, like this child. You find your significance not in your own self-absorbed, look-at-me, tower-building kingdom project, but in belonging to the family of the King, knowing that in His eyes you are never a failure, or insignificant.

John the Baptist gives us an example to follow. His life was taken up with pointing to Jesus. At one point he makes the statement,

> He must become greater; I must become less.[19]

Unlike the Corinthians or the city builders, John was taken up not with his own importance, but with pointing to the significance of Jesus alone.

Finding our significance in the eyes of the creator, we find we can lay down our heart agenda, of building cities of significance

---

18   Mark 9:35-37

19   John 3:30

with towers of self-idolatry. We can now serve God and point to Jesus. Let's stop the tiring, frantic, uncontrolled building, and find it all in the eyes of our Father. Only then can we in humility value others above ourselves, just as Jesus did,[20] and serve others and God completely.

---

20   Philippians 2:3-8

SUMMARY

Text & Focus: Genesis 11:4

> Then they said, 'Come, let us build ourselves a city, with a tower that reaches to the heavens, so that we may *make a name for ourselves*; otherwise we will be scattered over the face of the whole earth.'

Heart Agenda:	*Significance*
Heart Fear:	*Failure*
Heart Demand:	*'Make me look good!'*
	'Affirm my worth!'
	'Accept me!'
Heart Problem:	*Valuing God and others*

REFLECTION QUESTIONS

1. Is being a city builder a problem in your life?

2. In what areas of life do you look for significance?

3. What areas of life do you run from, fearing failure?

4. How do you try to get others to make you look good?

5. When do you require others to affirm you?

6. What do you do to try and get others to accept you?

7. Do you struggle to really value others and God?

Fire Lighters

3

Fire Lighters

The Story

The book of Isaiah transports us beyond the reigns of Saul, David and Solomon, to the time of the many kings of Judah and Israel in the divided kingdom. Israel and Judah's history had been a seesaw affair of trusting God or not. Some kings did, others didn't, relying rather on foreign powers or on their own military might to fight and find their way. Some are like Ahaz, who is depicted as wavering between standing firm in faith or following other alliances out of fear.[1] Others were like Hezekiah who, faced with the threat of a foreign army, stands firm trusting God to:

> Deliver ... so that all the kingdoms of the earth may know that you, LORD, are the only God.[2]

---

1   Isaiah 7:1-12
2   Isaiah 37:20

The two narratives of Ahaz and Hezekiah 'anchor the first half of the book [of Isaiah] demonstrating the importance of trust'[3] for the people of God.

But the people had again walked away from God and turned their backs on Him.[4] They had failed to keep their covenant of life with Yahweh, followed other gods, and seemingly entered into a covenant of death.[5] They had not heeded the many calls of God to return and trust Him, and now it appeared that they had been abandoned by God.[6] The kings of other nations had come against them, at times overrun them, and now Jerusalem itself had been destroyed and the people carried off to Babylon.[7] God had judged and disciplined them, but not completely forsaken them. Through the prophet Isaiah, God spoke of a need for repentance, the end of captivity, the return to Jerusalem, the restoration of the covenant people, and the sending of a saviour. They would yet be a light to the world.[8]

But would the people of Israel, now exiles by the river of Babylon, believe this promise of hope? Or would the loss of their city, a loss of significance, and the discipline of God be too much? Would they repent and return? Or would they simply walk away again?

God knew the battle in their hearts and gave His people these words in Isaiah 50:10-11, which immediately follows His promise of hope and restoration:

---

3   LaSor and Hubbard, *Old Testament Survey*, 294.

4   Isaiah 1:4

5   Isaiah 28:15,18

6   Isaiah 2:6

7   Isaiah 39:5-7

8   Isaiah 42:6-7, 49:8-18

Who among you fears the Lord and obeys the word of his servant? Let the one who walks in the dark, who has no light, trust in the name of the LORD and rely on their God. But now, all you who light fires and provide yourselves with flaming torches, go, walk in the light of your fires and of the torches you have set ablaze. This is what you shall receive from my hand: You will lie down in torment.

God's first question lays bare the hearts of the hearers in relation to their trust in God. 'Who among you fears the Lord?' In other words, even while you are in exile, and it appears that I have abandoned you, will you believe my promise of hope and deliverance, and put your trust in God alone? Or will you, like many of the kings before, waiver, and rely on your own strength, or seek help elsewhere? Interestingly the question is not left open to wide interpretation. The answer is to be backed up with specific evidence. 'Let the one who walks in the dark, who has no light, trust in the LORD, and rely on their God.' Therefore, the one who fears God is the one who trusts in the Lord during times of darkness.

What is the darkness that is being spoken of here? It's like in the time of Hezekiah, when an army was advancing against him, when things appeared hopeless and dark all around, he trusted God for deliverance and light, for a way through. The people believed that Yahweh was their God, that they were in the Promised Land and that the temple in Jerusalem was the place where God dwelt among them. But now, because they had rejected God, the temple had been destroyed by the Babylonians and they were exiled in a foreign land, surrounded by foreign gods. From their perspective God had completely abandoned them; they had been left in the dark. Yet now, the word of the Lord came saying that in the midst of their darkness and seemingly hopeless situation, there was light. There was a promise of salvation, of return, of restoration, of a future.[9] The people were being called to trust the words of God, through Isaiah, that there is hope, there is a future, there is a way through this uncertainty and darkness. Putting their solid trust in God's promise, no matter how difficult or unclear the circumstances may seem, is the evidence of a fearing heart that God seeks. This is the first group of people spoken of in these verses: those who trust despite the darkness.

But these verses also foresee another group of people who have a very different response. Namely, those who light fires and provide themselves with flaming torches. Who are these people? And what does it mean to light fires and provide yourself with flaming torches?

Providing yourself with flaming torches is clearly a reference to using your own strength and ingenuity to shed light on a dark situation and thereby find your own way out of any uncertainty you are facing. According to some,[10] the translation of 'providing yourself with flaming torches' needs strengthening. It is more like 'girding yourself with flaming torches'. It refers to an active preparation for battle, like fastening a torch onto your body so that you not only see the way ahead but also have your hands free, prepared for the fight. 'The picture here is of people seeking to equip themselves out of earthly resources to deal with earth's dark experiences. They feel the need of nothing they cannot

---

9   Isaiah 49

10   Motyer, *The Prophecy of Isaiah*, 401. Oswalt, *The Book of Isaiah Chapters 40-66*, 330.

generate for themselves.'[11] In other words, providing yourself with flaming torches is actively preparing and surrounding yourself with all that is required to make your own way out of any difficulty being faced. It is equipping yourself with everything necessary for obtaining success in life, without trust in God. It refers to those who prefer to live in certainty rather than by faith. These people are like the kings who had gone before, who chose to rely on their own strength, horses and resources, or made convenient foreign alliances, even bowing to other gods, in order to secure their pathway to the future. In the dark and desperate times of life they sought to manufacture their own pathway to salvation rather than trust the promises of God. For them certainty trumped faith almost every time.

There is a clear irony here. Those who find themselves in darkness and wish to walk in the certainty of their handmade light, rather than listening to and trusting God, will end up in torment and ultimate darkness. Perhaps their own torches, their own certainties, their own idols that they have strapped to themselves, will consume them. But those who find themselves in the darkness, and while having no light still trust in the Word of God and rely on Him, will receive deliverance, hope, and a future of never-ending light.

Fear the Lord and trust, or light your own fires and create your own destiny? Your choice.

Heart Agenda

The heart agenda of the fire lighter is certainty. They want everything to be clear, no mystery, no confusion, a step-by-step

---

11   Motyer, *The Prophecy of Isaiah*, 401.

process please, no need to trust, no walking by faith required. Just give me a torch to light the way. I will make it on my own.

But you say to me, how does all of this apply to us today? If we are not going into battle like the kings of long ago, and we don't appear to be in exile now, how do we light our own torches and create our own paths today? Let's take a closer look at what the kings were doing and see how that connects with our lives.

First, there is the darkness. The uncertainty of the battle was their darkness. Then there is the analysis. Spies are sent out to gather intelligence on the advancing enemy. How large was the opposition army? How many horses? How many soldiers? What were their weapons and armour? And so on. Then comes the comparison. How does the enemy army compare with theirs? Then there is the formulation of a strategy. Having gathered all the information they now consider the options. If they think they could win they go forward into battle. If they are unsure about the outcome, they seek other solutions, like building alliances, and then they develop their game plan and implement the strategy. They pick up their torches. They provide themselves with a way forward out of the darkness using their own planning, manipulation and resources. Of course the other option in situations like this, when all seems out of your control, is to trust God.

That was the uncertainty of battle. What about the uncertainty of exile? What was the present darkness of the exiles? Having lost their king, and their country, and most importantly their temple in Jerusalem, they thought they were without their God. Their darkness was their apparent abandonment by God, now seemingly lost and discarded as a people. Although, of course. they had abandoned God themselves. So God had now made their rejection of Him more obvious through removing the temple and sending them into exile in a foreign country, highlighting the actual distance they were from God and His promises in their hearts. Having rejected God and followed the gods of other lands and peoples, what use could they have for the temple and land of Yahweh? Would they not be more suited to the lands and temples of the gods they were worshipping? They were in a darkness of their own making, but in darkness, nevertheless.

Into this darkness God sends a promise. Now comes the analysis of the heart. What does the heart do? Trust in the promise of a return to the Promised Land, or make life work in a foreign land with foreign gods. So we question God. Has God been faithful to us in the past? Yes, but it does appear as if He has left us. Is this a real promise we can rely on? Maybe, but life is pretty good here; we have not been made to live as slaves like our ancestors were in Egypt under Pharaoh. We have been here a long time now and we are getting comfortable. Being here works – we know it, it's certain and it's not confusing. The promise seems less certain than the here and now. What is the strategy? Do we trust and rely on God and His promise, or put our faith in the certainty of our homes and our life, our torches, here in Babylon? Life here in Babylon seems more certain than another journey of faith, back to the Promised Land with God. Yes, Abraham did it, but can I trust like that?

We are no different. We love certainty, clarity and formulas to follow to a known end. Why do you think the books entitled, *The Five Steps to Success!* or *The Seven Keys to Being Highly Effective!* or *Ten Lessons for Fruitful Ministry!* or similar, catch your attention and sell so well? You want the answers, and you want them now. Quick, guaranteed and easy is what we want. Certainty, not trust, sells.

When our heart agenda is certainty, what does it do with God in the dark times of life? As I mentioned previously, we are currently suffering under the coronavirus pandemic that has cast its dark shadow across the entire world. We are in self-isolation, in lockdown, another form of exile. It affects everyone, young and old, weak and strong, rich and poor. We are all affected even if not infected. No one is immune from the problem. Whatever else it is, this worldwide pandemic of the coronavirus is a wake-up call. Darkness has come to all.

People are asking similar questions to the Israelites in exile in Babylon long ago. Now, like then, we scramble for answers, analysing the situation in search for certainty. We look around at the difficult situation, we see that things appear out of control, as if God has left us or doesn't care about us or is judging us. So we ask, 'What is God doing or saying through all of this?' But this is the wrong question. This question wants to do one of two things. Firstly, it wants to somehow link the virus to God's voice, as if He has specifically sent an additional curse on the world that is not linked to His original response to sin. Or, secondly, we try and gather some extra wisdom about what God is doing so that we can feed our desire for certainty, rather than our desire to walk daily by faith. Like Peter we look around and try to understand how to control the waves that surround us rather than trusting in the words of Christ.[12] In questioning God like this we are tempted to push God out of the picture believing that life is more certain if we trust in ourselves and our own resources.

The right question to ask in times of darkness is, 'What is our response to the situation we now find ourselves in?' Do

---

12   Matthew 14:22-32

we trust the promises, or are we afraid of the uncertainty and darkness, and tempted to grab a torch and make our own way through life, trusting in our resources and ingenuity? What is our strategy, our way ahead? If we are tempted to grab a torch what are we so afraid of?

Heart Fear

Why are we so afraid of the dark? Because it makes everything unclear. We can't see around or ahead with our own eyes. We lack certainty of movement and find ourselves in a place of confusion. We hate it! We are afraid of it. Where is our torch, our light, our way forward? We don't like those difficult circumstances in life where we are just stuck. Which university, which job, which relationship, which parenting style, which ministry approach? What do I do now? Can you feel it? Confusion. You hate it! And so do I. Someone, anyone, help me; tell me which way to go, tell me what to do. Stuck, just like those in exile, confused. Do we wait for God, trusting? It's so hard to wait, isn't it? Because we are not sure, we are not certain. Of what? Whether God has forgotten us? Whether He will show up and show us the way? Or whether we will like the way He gives us if and when He shows up?

The Israelites at another time struggled with this same problem. They wanted certainty, they thought God had forgotten them, so after waiting a short while, when they could bear it no longer, they chose another way, their fire lighter way. It was in the desert at Mount Sinai.

> When the people saw that Moses was so long in coming down from the mountain, they gathered around Aaron and said, 'Come, make us gods who will go before us. As for this fellow

Moses who brought us up out of Egypt, we don't know what has happened to him.'

Aaron answered them, 'Take off the gold earrings that your wives, your sons and your daughters are wearing, and bring them to me.' So all the people took off their earrings and brought them to Aaron.

He took what they handed him and made it into an idol cast in the shape of a calf, fashioning it with a tool. Then they said, 'These are your gods, Israel, who brought you up out of Egypt.' When Aaron saw this, he built an altar in front of the calf and announced, 'Tomorrow there will be a festival to the LORD.' So the next day the people rose early and sacrificed burnt offerings and presented fellowship offerings. Afterward they sat down to eat and drink and got up to indulge in revelry.[13]

Moses had gone up the mountain to talk with God, to receive instructions about the law and how to build the tabernacle that God would come and dwell in among His people. After forty days the patience of the people had run out. Their leader and their God had apparently disappeared, at least in their minds. After such a short amount of time, confusion and uncertainty set in. Their way forward had disappeared. What would they do now? They would find another way. They would find their own way forward. They would create another god to lead them on, one that couldn't even see. Yet they said of the idols they created, 'These are your gods, Israel, who brought you up out of Egypt.' Had they forgotten the exodus already? Had they forgotten the Passover meal and their deliverance from Pharaoh? Had they forgotten the impossible escape through the Red Sea? Had they forgotten the provision and the presence of God? How quickly they had forgotten all this in their moment of darkness

---

13   Exodus 32:1-6

and uncertainty. In their fear and confusion, they had chosen to light their own torches, and provide their own way, their own certain way, away from God.

I had an impression: not a voice, just an impression. I thought it was from God. I checked with my wife and we both agreed that somehow God was calling us onto a different path. It's important that you know that if my wife, Judy, doesn't think God is involved then it's normally just one of my many hair-brained ideas. Not to say they are bad, but just that they are not part of a message from God. So it seemed to us that God was calling us into some form of church ministry. In my mind I thought it would play out that I would work part time for our church, for little remuneration, and part time elsewhere in the accounting or management sphere to support our family. We had a significant mortgage which we felt we needed to reduce, to decrease our financial commitment, and therefore minimize our required level of income. So we put the house on the market, excited about this new adventure with God. We waited for interested buyers. And we waited. And waited. Come on, God, what are you doing? Did we get it wrong; you mean you don't want us to sell our house and serve you in ministry? Or more patience? For eighteen months. Nothing. Not one enquiry. Darkness, confusion.

Finally a breakthrough. Not a buyer but an incidental comment. In the middle of an otherwise undramatic moment, someone asked how the house selling was going, and so I told them there was no action on that front. Then, they said matter-of-factly, 'Why don't you rent the house and go to Bible College?' Well, this statement was like a lightning bolt out of heaven. Or maybe thunder because I can still hear it today. *That's it,* I thought. God doesn't want us to go straight into ministry, He wants us to be trained. So we put the house up for rent, and we made enquiries. Which college? What course? How long? How much will it cost? What funding is available? When do the semesters start? All the usual questions. The analysis in the midst of the obvious uncertainty.

I'm logical in my thinking so I thought it through, logically. We needed a renter, or buyer, and we needed a date to leave my work and travel to the college. Living in Tasmania I knew that our move would be to the mainland,[14] and so travel and removalists would be involved. I also wanted to know whether there was any government funding available for us while we were studying. In other words, could we afford to go? Soon after we found a renter who would also buy the house in a year's time. We found the right course and college in Perth, Western Australia, so I applied. I wrote to the government department asking for confirmation of funding approval.[15] I set the dates that I would communicate my decision to the church and resign from my job, so we would have enough time to leave work, pack up, and drive across the breadth of Australia, to Perth. The dates were set. I would tell the church on Sunday, December 1, 1996, and resign the following day.

The day approached. I was accepted into the college, and the rental contract was signed. But no word from the government. No certainty surrounding the funding. The Friday arrived, but no letter came. Saturday, decision day. God, what are you doing? You have confirmed everything else, why not the finances?

---

14 The mainland is what Tasmanians call the rest of Australia.

15 If you are reading this from another country, you may wonder why I was asking the government about funding. But in Australia the government provides a means tested family living allowance for people who are studying approved courses.

What am I supposed to do now? Do I in faith, announce on Sunday and resign Monday? Or do I hold onto my job and wait for certainty? Trust or certainty? Sunday came as it generally does, and I announced we were leaving the church to go to Perth Bible College. I went to work on Monday and told my boss the same story. Done, no turning back now.

That Monday, after resigning, I went home and looked in the letter box, and there it was, the letter I had been waiting for. It confirmed the funding was approved. Remember this was before email, so the letter was posted on the Friday before I announced and resigned, but I did not receive it until the Monday afternoon, after all announcements had been made. God, why? Yes, I was pleased to know the funding was coming but God why couldn't the letter have come on Friday to make everything certain? My heart agenda. Why did you leave me hanging, in confusion about what to do for so long? Why did you have to test my faith, so I had to trust in you? You know I dislike uncertainty; I like everything to be clear.

Heart Demand

Take a journey inside your heart. What do you find? Faith and trust, patience and peace, or a deep desire for certainty and a fear of confusion and mystery? Stop and ask yourself, 'How does my life work?' Or better still, given that surely no one denies that this world is uncertain, let's ask, 'How do I make my life work in this unpredictable and complicated world?' In other words, according to what agenda do I manage my life? What is my heart demand?

My heart wants the letter to arrive before critical decisions need to be made. My heart wants this coronavirus pandemic to leave, for the lockdown to lift, and for life to get back to normal.

My heart wants to know the right gift to buy my wife, the right car to buy my daughter, the right holiday options for the family. Why? I demand certainty, not confusion. I don't want the darkness of these situations; I want my pathway lit up and clear. Why? If I'm really honest it's because I want life to work out my way, according to my plans, to ensure the best possible outcome. I want others, including God, to get in on the act of supporting my agenda. If I'm honest I will use them rather than serve them, to achieve my agenda. And if they won't serve to help make my life more certain and successful, then it would be more beneficial for me if they just get out of my way so I can grab my own torch and get on with doing it all on my own. That's it; I demand that God and others serve me by helping make my life certain. That's my heart demand.

While we are busy demanding, we want the support from others to come to us in two ways. Firstly, when we come across a problem or a crossroad, or need to make a significant decision, we need people to support us in our investigation process. We ask around, as many people as we can find, to find out what their thoughts are on the subject. I'm not saying don't ask around for good advice, but to think about why we are asking. Do we ask because we don't want to be responsible for making mistakes? Often, we ask because we want others to share the load, to tell us what is going to work. We want others to give us ideas about what the best way ahead might be. We don't want the responsibility, but we want the certainty. We want to follow their formula, their pathway, their solution; we want their torchlight. We do this with the small unimportant things. 'What do you think about this outfit? Will it work?' 'Tell me it will work!' We want problem-free fashion. We do it with the more important decisions. 'What do you think about our engagement?' 'Please tell me it will work!' 'I have done the right thing, haven't I?' We want problem-free relationships. We do it with matters of life, 'Tell me, what is the best way to bring up my children? I'm so uncertain, I need answers!' We want problem-free children. We do it with our health. We've all heard people say, 'It's the not knowing that is the hardest!' 'Please tell me what the problem is then I will know what to do!' And we do it with aspects of ministry. 'You are doing well. What is your secret formula to growing your church?' We all want certain pathways forward. We demand of God or others if He won't oblige, 'Tell me what will work! And can you do it now, please?'

Secondly, we find ourselves looking for people to support us by agreeing with us. When we are working through a significant issue, problem or decision and have already demanded the opinions of others and somehow come to a resolution, we move to phase two of the heart demand. We now want people to agree with our decision. To get rid of the remaining uncertainty we ask, 'This is the right way, isn't it?' We try and express this with as much certainty as we can muster, but if we are honest we always know that it ends with an echo of doubt. And to remove this lingering doubt we ask others to affirm our choice, our selected path, and our torch of choice. Sometimes we go as far as trying to convince others that our choice is right, so that when they agree with us we ourselves can be fully convinced that we are right. How crazy is that! We convince others to convince us so that we are convinced. Madness!

I have worked in church leadership for many years and have trained people for ministry of many types. In ministry, once you get over yourself and the ugly idol of significance, you run headlong into the idol of certainty in its many manifestations. The questions of 'What is the answer?' 'How do I deal with this?'

'What is the best way?' never stop. And it's not that it's wrong to ask these questions; you must, otherwise you don't learn. But the point is what do you do when there is no definitive answer to your question? Demand certainty? Seek a formula, and light you own fire? Or be patient, be faithful and trust? Right here certainty is connected to significance. Your search and demand for an effective formula to follow is designed to give you not only certainty, but guaranteed success, and thereby greater significance. Two idols joined as one.

A preacher wants the formula to amass and capture the attention of a crowd. An evangelist wants the recipe to quick church growth. A pastoral carer wants the best model for healing through wise counsel. A treasurer wants the guaranteed way of inciting generosity and obtaining that elusive surplus.

I have worked with people who believe that faithfulness in lean times is not enough. There must be more. Their desire for success and significance, coupled with their fear of failure, and their growing impatience launches a certainty quest – a search for the latest trend, the latest programme, the latest release. All the time they are asking others, 'What is the best way you have found?' or 'What do you think of this approach?' They are continuously demanding certainty in the midst of their confusion, looking for a quick pathway out of the darkness. We hear the clear echoes of the demands 'Tell me what will work!' and 'Agree with me!' All the while they are searching for a solution to solve the problem, which is reaching for a torch, hoping to end the frustration. Confusion plus a lack of patience seems to lead to fire lighting. And sadly, and somewhat ironically, many in ministry burn out here. Their quest is sustained for a while; it may even appear spiritual, they appear so 'on fire' and enthusiastic. In their noise and flurry of action they try to convince others that they are on the right path. Not to be left out or to look foolish you give in to their demands. Or sometimes to get them to be quiet so you can rest for a while, in exhaustion you just agree with them. Then you wake up and realize that by reluctantly agreeing, you have given them the torch. They can now light the fire, feeling they have found at last some certainty to push back the darkness. But it doesn't last; formulas in ministry rarely do. The questions and uncertainties return once more, and with greater force. They have tried all the options, there are no quick or certain solutions to be found and they are left feeling alone, in confusion and darkness, a failure. The enthusiasm vanishes, the fire dies out and the quest is lost. They come to the end of themselves. Burnt out.

However, in contrast there is James. We were sitting on the couch in my office sharing a coffee and discussing the plans for our annual mission trip to Africa. The previous year we had run pastors' training conferences in Kampala, Uganda and in Khartoum, Sudan. At the end of our time in Uganda we had visited a refugee camp called Palabek, in northern Uganda close to the border of South Sudan. Following our time of preaching our discussion turned to the possibility of trusting God to be able to run a pastors' training conference in Gulu, the closest regional centre. The conference would be for training the pastors from the many refugee camps that were spreading and growing across the Uganda/South Sudan border. Over coffee we reminded each other of this conversation and discussed the possibility. James had just received an estimate for what hosting a conference in Gulu for around 100 pastors would cost. We needed to supply transport from the camps, accommodation for four nights, food for three days, as well as covering our own costs. It was a lot. It would double the cost of the mission trip compared to the previous year. So we needed to find double the support. 'Could we do it?' was what I was thinking. See the subtle underlying question, 'Tell me, will it work?' I knew this was a faith moment, but in my subtle search for more certainty I asked James, 'If it will cost this much, do you think we should go to Gulu and run this conference for the South Sudanese pastors?' A fair question which I thought would be met with a well-reasoned logical response. Instead James just said, 'It's already happened!' I didn't understand his response, so I asked, 'What do you mean by, it's already happened?' He said, 'Well, in situations like this we only need to answer two questions. Does God want this to happen? And are we prepared to trust God and be part of it?' He continued, 'The answer to the first one is easy. Of course God wants the pastors of the refugee camps to be trained. Then all we must do is decide whether we will trust God and be part of it. So if we trust Him and want to be part of it, and if God wants it done, then it's just like it's already happened.' I was stunned by the simplicity and certainty of his trust.

So we did trust, we did go, and God did provide, in ways above and beyond our imagination. Just trust, and if God wants it, it's already happened. Suddenly trust seems like the best kind of certainty, and darkness with God brighter than the light of our own torches.

Heart Problem

While our heart agenda is certainty, our corresponding heart problem is trust. Our desire for certainty and our fear of confusion, leads to a heart that is unwilling to trust God and others. It's like Adam and Eve in the garden, listening to the serpent say, 'Did God really say?'[16] then acting as if the serpent told the truth and God could not be trusted. Like Adam and Eve our heart wants to take control and provide its own way for the future. Because relying on God and others seems so uncertain, we trust in self.

This was certainly true for the Israelites, who had forgotten so quickly the plagues, the Passover, the exodus, the food and water, the visible presence of God in the desert day and night. All forgotten in the silence of a moment. Our hearts don't want to trust an invisible God and a lost prophet; we want a visible idol to follow, just like they had back in Egypt. The temptation of the certainty of the old life grew and overwhelmed the call to trust God in the new. How quickly they lit their torches and headed for certain destruction.[17]

Those in exile in Babylon had the same problem. Trust the certainty of a life in a foreign land, with foreign gods, or trust that the God who had sent them into exile, left the temple and allowed it to be destroyed, had from the silence spoken again. Would they trust the God of the prophet, the God of the promise – the promise of a new future back in the Promised Land? The torch or trust? Your own fire or faith?

What do you do in the dark uncertain times of life? Choose the voice of the Lord and His promises, being content to endure the sometimes uncertain, dark and confusing times of life, placing trust in God alone? Or, afraid of such darkness, you seek to avoid any uncertainty and confusion, by resourcefully setting out on your own path, with your own torch, creating your own light?

---

16   Genesis 3:1

17   Exodus 32:35

Or maybe like many others you believe that certainty and light, rather than darkness and uncertainty equates to the blessings of God. If all is clear, and all is going well, then that is the light of the gospel and the abundant life, right? Not so! You have most likely combined blessing and certainty to form your own idea of light, and your own idea of abundant life. We must be so careful here. Blessings and certainty may have nothing to do with true light and true life and could quite possibly have everything to do with fire lighting. We so easily deceive ourselves, believing that our idea of a good life is the same as God's will for us. When actually all we are doing is projecting our heart's desires onto God's to-do list.

You could be forgiven for thinking that 'To fear and obey the voice of the Servant would seem to imply having an abundance of light. But on reflection this is not necessarily the case. Those who follow this Servant may indeed walk with him into the darkness of frustration, injustice, humiliation, and abuse'[18] that He Himself suffered. The Christian life does not guarantee certainty, but trouble.[19] It guarantees a full life conformed to Christ; a life that includes humility, suffering and trouble. Yet in the same troublesome verse there is an offer of peace.

Peace comes in trusting Christ alone, not in trusting our own ways or our own ideas of the good life. The question is whether our agenda for control and certainty will swamp our faith and trust in God? The natural agenda for our heart is to desire certainty. Our heart's desire for certainty always takes us a step away from faith. And a step away from faith toward our own certainty is always a step away from God toward self. God

18   Oswalt, *The Book of Isaiah Chapters 40-66*, 329.

19   John 16:33

is looking for you to have faith in the midst of the darkness. He was looking for it from the Israelites in the desert, in the exile, and He is looking for it from us now.

Does your fear of uncertainty drive your life and move you toward self-reliance? Or do you enjoy the intimacy and peace that comes from faith and trust? Are you always trying to figure everything out and require others to help you or to agree with you? Are you demanding that life work your way, according to your torch rather than trust? Are you always busy creating your own fires to light up your way? It seems obvious, but you don't need faith or God for that matter when you have your own light.

God's Heart Agenda

My heart wants to order my life. God wants through life to order my heart. Certainty or 'my way' orders my life for me. Trust or God's way orders my life for God.

But do I hear you say, 'God, why couldn't the letter have come on Friday to make everything certain?' That is the voice of my heart. I think God says, 'The letter came on Monday to give you the opportunity to show me that you trust me. It was in the mail over the weekend to show you that while you were in darkness and uncertainty, I was thinking about you. I wanted to show you that I was acting on your behalf, that I loved you, and that it had already happened.'

Back at Sinai while the Israelites were lighting their torches, melting gold in furnaces, creating idols, and indulging in revelry, what were God and Moses doing on the mountain? At the same time that His children were running away from Him, creating their own paths, God was delivering the plans for the tabernacle. God was taking the forty days and nights to show Moses how to prepare a place in which He would come and dwell among His people. God wanted to be with His people, to be their light in the darkness, to be their certainty in the confusing wilderness. But they couldn't wait. They couldn't trust any longer; they needed a light, any light, an idol, any idol.

To those in exile, through Isaiah He gave a word of hope to all who would listen and trust, beyond all the darkness that surrounded them in the foreign land. That hope was that the Messiah would come; He would dwell with them, forgive their sins and make all things new. He did come, after more silence, 400 years of it in fact. He came in Jesus, to dwell among us.

He has also promised that He is coming again, to be with you, fully and finally. You may think that He is silent. You may think He is not interested in you. You may think that His promises cannot be counted on, that He doesn't have your best interests at heart and that He has left you in the dark. It's your choice now, torch or trust? But before you grab that torch and find your own way in life, ask yourself 'What is God doing now?' To answer this we must go back to the upper room.

Jesus came. He lived for a number of years with the disciples. They learned to follow Him. They learned to believe in Him. He provided certainty and light in their otherwise uncertain, oppressed and dark world. But then in the late hours and candlelight of the upper room, following His lesson on significance and service Jesus says He is going to leave them. Peter as always was first in, 'Lord, where are you going?' Jesus replied, 'Where I am going, you cannot follow now, but you will follow later.'[20] All of a sudden what was certain for the disciples was now replaced by confusion. This news naturally upset them. They couldn't bear the thought of Jesus leaving them after

---

20   John 13:36

spending almost every moment of the past three years with them. Fear was rising in their hearts. They must have thought 'This can't be right. You are the Messiah. You have come to overthrow the Romans and to set everything right, just as the promises say. And we will be there to serve in your kingdom, right at your side. We are prepared to even die for this certain and significant dream.' Or was it just their torch, their idea, their certainty? Now they were shaken, lost and fearful of being left alone without their leader. They were plunged into uncertainty, now not knowing what was going to happen. All of a sudden, a breath of cool evening air crossed the upper room. They shivered and the candle flickered; it was almost gone.

As the candle steadied, they pondered. They knew Jesus was the Son of God, so why would He leave them? And what did 'you will follow later' mean? Jesus knew their hearts; He knew their agenda and their fear, so He gave them words of comfort, calling for them to trust in the midst of their fear and anxiety. In John 14:1-3 we read that Jesus said to the disciples:

> Do not let your hearts be troubled. Trust in God; trust also in me. In my Father's house are many rooms; if it were not so, I would have told you. I am going there to prepare a place for you. And if I go and prepare a place for you, I will come back and take you to be with me that you also may be where I am.

When we read these words, to us they immediately convey the fact that Jesus is coming back to take us to be with Him one day, and so we should trust. But to the disciples, in their moment of fear, I think they meant so much more.

In ancient times, and in some cultures still today, when a young man reached the age to marry, he would not start looking for a wife; his father would do the looking for him. The father would scout around the village or further into other towns and villages across the region, searching for a suitable young lady to be his son's bride. When he had found the right one, the two families and all their relatives and friends would gather at the home of the bride for a huge engagement celebration.

Engagement in those days was different to today. Today, in Australia, when you get engaged you are promising to marry someone at a future time. If you break off the engagement, while still often considered as a shock or disappointment by many, it is not viewed as a huge life mistake. But in Jesus' time when you became engaged you and your chosen one were making a covenant with each other. You were considered to be effectively married; there was no option of breaking the engagement, as that would be considered on a par with divorce. So, an engagement celebration carried with it the seriousness of today's marriage, except the two did not begin to live together straight after the celebrations. At the end of the engagement celebration the groom and his family left the bride and her extended family and returned to their village. The groom would not see his bride again until the day of the wedding. What was the young bride to do while the groom was away? Trust for the return.

What was the groom doing while he was away from his bride? He would go back to the land of his family and begin building a home for his bride and their anticipated family.

In those days people lived in extended family groups, with each living on a different part of the family land or in a separate section of the family dwelling. When a son was to be married the family would simply add an extension onto their existing structure or build a new home on a section of their land to accommodate him and his new bride.

So the groom arrived home to begin the building project and prepare a place for his bride. He would not see his bride face to face or return for her until the project was complete.

The bride was not surprised to see her groom depart the engagement celebrations. She knew that as sure as he went, their engagement covenant meant that he would return to take her home to be with him one day. She would trust and make herself ready for the day of his return. She had no idea how long he would take to make the home. If he was a good builder, he might not take too long. If he was not, it might take a while. While she waited, trusting in the promise of his return, she would prepare herself for the day that he would come back and take her away to live with him. She knew he was coming and could trust in that. The return was certain; she would not be caught unprepared.

She would also be completely overcome with the excitement of the anticipation of the groom's return. I think if you saw such a woman who was anticipating such an exciting event you could not help but notice that there was something different about her. It was probably all she talked about. She wasn't concerned with building a life for herself in her village; all she did was related to the return and the anticipation of the certain future with her husband in his home. Her trust in her returning groom gave her a clear and definite purpose and her whole being would have radiated the hope that now resided within her. Her trust in the future return gave her certainty and a life worth living to the full.

The disciples on hearing these words from Jesus knew without confusion that He was going, but also that He promised to return like a groom would return for his bride. He was going to prepare a place for them and would come back one day to take them there. They would have to wait here for a while, and trust. But they knew their trust would turn into certain reality upon the return of the groom, when Jesus would take them to be with Him, to live in close relationship with Him, in the home of the Father, forever. What an incredible joy and hope for them!

What about us? We have the same promise, the same hope. Jesus came and has gone back, just as the groom did, and is preparing a place for us to be with Him, in the home of the Father. A place that we will share with Him forever. What a hope we have!

I wonder if, like the bride in the story, our faces show the same certain hope that hers did? I wonder if our whole life is determined by the promise we have of His return? Does it consume our time? Is it what we talk to others about? Can people look at us and know that something exciting and certain has gripped us, changed our life, and given us real purpose?

Could the Israelites in the desert, in the absence of God and Moses, trust and wait? Did those in exile in Babylon, in the silence and confusion, trust and wait? Would the disciples, amidst the difficulties, opposition and persecution that came, trust and wait? Do we, in the uncertainty of our times, in the moments when God seems quiet and all seems dark, trust and wait?

The groom does return. When the home is ready – the curtains hung, the carpets laid, and everything just right – he returns to the town of his bride. He and his family come for the wedding feast. Out in front of the groom's family group, as they travel toward the bride's town, are servants who blow their horns and make a noise. A noise that lets the people of the bride's town know that the groom is coming, so that they should be ready to welcome the groom and begin the wedding celebrations. Finally, the groom meets up with his bride and the families celebrate the couple's long-awaited union. At the end of the marriage feast the bride and groom return to the groom's hometown, to the family estate to reside in the new rooms built just for them.

Jesus, who gave His life for us, who left the disciples 2000 years ago, is preparing now a place for us, and He will return for us as a groom returns for his bride. One day we will hear a great noise, and we will be ushered into the wedding celebrations of the church and Jesus Christ.

> Then I heard what sounded like a great multitude, like
> the roar of rushing waters and like loud peals of thunder,
> shouting:
>> 'Hallelujah!
>> For our Lord God Almighty reigns.
> Let us rejoice and be glad
>> and give him glory!
>> For the wedding of the Lamb has come,
>> and his bride has made herself ready.'[21]

God's heart agenda for us is to trust in such a certain future, in the midst of the not so certain present, and be ready, without fear, trusting Him.

Monicah expresses something of having discovered this heart of trust through much suffering and trouble. Monicah comes from the Dinka tribe of South Sudan. A few years ago, she left her family and fled with others to Kenya, to avoid the war in South Sudan, seeking a safer life. As a South Sudanese refugee in Kenya she is not given the same rights as citizens of Kenya. She could attend primary school but was not allowed to attend a public high school. I met Monicah for the first time in 2016, and as a family we have helped Monicah gain a high

---

21   Revelation 19:6-7

school education in a Christian school in Kenya. In October of 2019, Monicah lost her father who was living in Juba, the capital of South Sudan. He was beaten and left to die during an attack by another tribe. He died because he was not able to access appropriate medical facilities.

I met up with Monicah for the second time on my trip to Africa in December 2019. During our conversations she shared this extract from her journal.

> Dad, you are no more. I will never be able to see you again on this earth. You have gone too soon, when I never expected it. Your absence in my life weighs so heavy on me. People tell me to be strong. But they don't know that the strongest feeling in me is wanting to be with you again, and this feeling threatens to tear me apart. What pains me most is the pain I saw you go through. If only I had the ability to share the pain with you, it would have been my joy. Dad, rest in eternal peace.

Monicah goes on to address God in the midst of the darkness of her grief.

> God, I will always remember that you told me that I should not run away from the difficulties in my life. These problems you have said are not random mistakes, but they are hand-tailored blessings designed for my benefit and growth. You have told me that I should embrace all the circumstances that you allow in my life, trusting you to bring good out of them. You have told me to view problems as opportunities to rely more fully on you. You have also told me that when I want to start to feel stressed, I should let those feelings alert me of my need for you. You have promised that my needs are a doorway to deep dependence on you, and that increases intimacy between us. Although self-sufficiency is acclaimed in

the world, you have said reliance on you produces abundant living in your kingdom. Thanking is what you have said to do for the difficulties in my life, since they provide protection from the idolatry of self-reliance.[22]

God is constantly teaching us to trust, seeking to move us away from the idolatry of certainty and self-reliance. This is what He wants for us. He doesn't want to have to say to us, 'Go, walk in the light of your own fires and flaming torches and see where it takes you – into torment!'

To take the words of wisdom we are to trust in the Lord with all our heart and lean not on our own understanding. And if we acknowledge Him in all our ways, He will make our paths straight. [23] Without lighting fires, we are to patiently trust the one who is the light. No torch. Just trust. Remember, the one who fears the Lord is the one who trusts in the one who is the light, during times of darkness, knowing that the darkness will not overcome it.[24]

---

22   Used with permission – Monicah Malith Nyareng

23   Proverbs 3:5-6

24   John 1:5

Summary

Text & Focus: Isaiah 50:10-11

Who among you fears the Lord and obeys the word of his servant? Let the one who walks in the dark, who has no light, trust in the name of the Lord and rely on their God. But now, *all you who light fires* and provide yourselves with flaming torches, go, walk in the light of your fires and of the torches you have set ablaze. This is what you shall receive from my hand: You will lie down in torment.

Heart Agenda:	*Certainty*
Heart Fear:	*Confusion*
Heart Demand:	*'Tell me what will work!'*
	'Agree with me!'
Heart Problem:	*Trusting God and others*

Reflection Questions

1. Is being a fire lighter a problem in your life?

2. In what areas of life do you look for certainty?

3. What areas of life do you feel uncomfortable or stressed, fearing confusion and uncertainty?

4. In what life circumstances do you try and get people to agree with you?

5. When do you require others to tell you what will work?

6. In what areas do you struggle with self-reliance?

7. Do you struggle to really trust others and God?

Whitewashers

4

Whitewashers

The Story

The book of Ezekiel takes us back again to Babylon. Nebuchadnezzar had captured Jerusalem and taken control of the Promised Land. Ezekiel, who came from a priestly family, had been transported east in 597 B.C. in one of the early deportations from Jerusalem to Babylon. He and his wife were now living in a Jewish community of new exile arrivals called Tel Aviv, just outside the main city of Babylon, beside the Kebar River.[1]

For years, and through many prophets, God had been telling His people that unless they turned back to Him they would be punished and sent into exile, and Jerusalem, the temple, and the land would be destroyed. But would they listen? No. After all, they thought, they were God's people. They had been

---

1   Ezekiel 1:1, 3:15, 24:16

punished before; other nations had risen and had overrun them. But God had always come to their aid, in some way or another He had always rescued and restored them. After all, this was the Promised Land, the land promised to Abraham, Isaac and Jacob, the land restored under Moses and Joshua. God had chosen to dwell here among His chosen people. His home was in Jerusalem, in the temple, above the Ark of the Covenant, between the cherubim. God would not judge them and their land and send them into exile, or so they thought.

So what does God do? He sends Ezekiel and instructs him to be a very different prophet. Apparently just speaking to the people before wasn't enough, so this time God was going to mix it up. Ezekiel is commissioned as a prophet to deliver God's words of warning and judgement again, but this time he is to do it with a twist, for the visual learners. He is to be the first theatrical prophet, a living dramatic sign. God gives him a message and he is to act it out in full view of the exiled Israelites.

Questions obviously arose within the exile community on the outskirts of Babylon. 'What will happen next?' 'What will happen to the rest of the people left in the Promised Land?' 'What will happen to Jerusalem?' 'What will happen to the temple?' And most importantly, 'What is God going to do?'

Into the midst of this situation God brings Ezekiel. He was not only instructed by God to act out His messages to the exiles, but was struck dumb by God, unable to speak to the people, or on behalf of the people, until many of the dramatic acts had been fulfilled.[2] Ezekiel's theatrical performance to the audience of the first exiles in Babylonia opened with the siege of the walls of Jerusalem. It continued with scenes dramatizing the pending

---

2   Ezekiel 3:26, 24:27

years of exile, the starvation of those left after the overthrow of Jerusalem, the smallness of the remnant who would escape the judgement, and their eventual destiny, being added to the number in exile. After a performance break Ezekiel returned to continue the drama, adding scenes depicting the march of the Babylonians to Jerusalem, the departing of God from the temple, and the final fall, destruction, and burning of Jerusalem, including the temple, the house of God. The final scene coming with added emphasis through Ezekiel losing that which was dearest to him, his wife.

What a play! The intended message for those in exile was to realize that they had rejected God, and that God was going to quickly move to send the Babylonians to judge the people and the land. That God would depart from His home in the temple and allow it and the city to be completely destroyed, with only a few survivors being carried off into exile to join them.

They were stunned. They thought, 'Would God actually do this?' They figured, 'This is our God; He has always come to our aid and has always been there to rescue us, to get us out of a crisis. The temple is His house; He won't leave that. And He won't leave the Promised Land, the land promised to Abraham, Isaac and Jacob, the land that Moses and Joshua led the people back into to reclaim, the land that He built His temple and city in, and the land that He had dwelt in and protected for generation after generation. He wouldn't, He couldn't. Could He? It's one thing to send us into exile, it's quite another for God to abandon the land, city, and temple.' They thought that Ezekiel had got it all wrong, that he had gone completely mad, and that his performances were just that, dramatized fiction.

After all, they concluded, 'Even if these things are true, God will not act quickly.' They remembered their proverb that had developed over the years as prophets purporting to have visions of pending judgement and exile had come and gone. They repeated it to each other to build a sense of security, 'The days go by and every vision comes to nothing.'[3] They said it repeatedly. Ezekiel has gone mad; we, the temple, the city and the land are safe. Nothing is going to happen, at least not soon.

But just to be sure, because they weren't, they went to get further advice, a second opinion, from other prophets. These false prophets assured the enquirers that their proverb would continue to serve them well. They said, 'The vision Ezekiel sees is for many years from now, and he prophesies about the distant future.'[4] In other words, don't worry; be happy!

However, in response to the people's complacency and denial the sovereign Lord said to Ezekiel, 'None of my words will be delayed any longer, whatever I say will be fulfilled...' God was about to fulfil the prophecies, put an end to the proverb that they hid behind, and destroy the false prophets that they consulted. In Ezekiel 13:8-16 God proclaims:

> Therefore this is what the Sovereign Lord says: Because of your false words and lying visions, I am against you, declares the Sovereign Lord. My hand will be against the prophets who see false visions and utter lying divinations. They will not belong to the council of my people or be listed in the records of Israel, nor will they enter the land of Israel. Then you will know that I am the Sovereign Lord.
>
> Because they lead my people astray, saying, 'Peace', when there is no peace, and because, when a flimsy wall is built, they cover it with whitewash, therefore tell those who cover it with

---

3   Ezekiel 12:22

4   Ezekiel 12:27

whitewash that it is going to fall. Rain will come in torrents, and I will send hailstones hurtling down, and violent winds will burst forth. When the wall collapses, will people not ask you, 'Where is the whitewash you covered it with?'

Therefore this is what the Sovereign LORD says: In my wrath I will unleash a violent wind, and in my anger hailstones and torrents of rain will fall with destructive fury. I will tear down the wall you have covered with whitewash and will level it to the ground so that its foundation will be laid bare. When it falls, you will be destroyed in it; and you will know that I am the LORD. So I will pour out my wrath against the wall and against those who covered it with whitewash. I will say to you, 'The wall is gone and so are those who whitewashed it, those prophets of Israel who prophesied to Jerusalem and saw visions of peace for her when there was no peace, declares the Sovereign LORD.'

God is not delaying; He is acting. Not only will He destroy the prophets, He is going to destroy a whitewashed wall as well. In this passage a flimsy wall is built, covered with whitewash, and then destroyed. This picture is the key to what is going on in the hearts and minds of the people and the false prophets in exile.

Ezekiel's message wasn't new. He had been affirming what other true prophets of Israel had been saying for years. God will judge His people, destroy the temple and the city, and send them into exile, because of their sin and rebellion. But the people hadn't listened. Perhaps they believed that a good God could not abandon His land, His temple, and His people, the way Ezekiel was describing? Perhaps it was the potency of the proverb and the time delays? Nothing immediate seemed to happen after the previous prophets had spoken. Perhaps they were echoing the words of their previous king? After being forewarned of the pending destruction of Jerusalem by the prophet Isaiah, Hezekiah was recorded to have said 'There will be peace and security in my lifetime.'[5] Or perhaps it was a combination of all three: disbelief, complacency and self-deception. From the words of the false prophets, the proverbs of their forefathers, and the thoughts of a prominent king, the people had built a wall of protection around themselves. A flimsy wall created from the imagination of fortune-tellers.[6] A weak wall manufactured out of the superstitions of the past. A wall of deceptive peace fabricated in the face of pending destruction. A wall whitewashed with proverbs, lies and imagination, erected to create an alternative reality to hide behind. A wall to keep disaster and God at bay. A wall behind which faith is not tested. A decorated wall behind which comfort, security, and self-interests are protected, where crisis is denied or averted.

A wall is created for a purpose. In the historical context of our passage a wall would normally be created to protect a city, to keep it safe and secure. The thicker, higher and stronger the wall, the more protected and secure the citizens of the city would feel. The wall we have described here is weak and whitewashed, or painted. It is whitewashed to make it look like it is something of substance when it is clearly not. It is weak, made to look strong. It is pretence, dressed up as security. On the outside it puts up a good show, but underneath it will not stand the test. This is exactly what we see in the passage next. A real test in the form of a storm comes and the wall falls and is gone. All those that think God will not allow Jerusalem and the temple to fall and be destroyed are about to get a real surprise. It's going to happen.

---

5   Isaiah 39:8

6   Ezekiel 13:2

The security of a false idea of God will be replaced by the reality of coming judgement and disaster. No more whitewash, no more flimsy wall to hide behind. No more cover-up of reality with fantasy. All will be smashed and laid bare. And then what will they do? Abandon God? These words spoken by Ezekiel around 597 B.C. were fulfilled with the destruction of Jerusalem in 587 B.C.

Heart Agenda

The heart agenda of a whitewasher is peace, safety and security. They live under the false belief that God will not allow any disaster to befall a Christian. They believe that all things work together for good, meaning that all things should work together for their idea of good, which includes a comfortable, problem-free life.

Whitewashers don't want to hear any bad news. They are the original ostriches with their heads in the sand. They are always looking for good news avoiding the bad. They are experts at pointing out the silver lining that surrounds the pending storm. In conversation they change the subject to cover up possible trouble with humour, they replace heavy darkness with the lightness of whitewash. They are constantly figuring out how they can avoid any potential problem, crisis or disaster. They are skilled at denying and avoiding difficulties at all costs, and if that is not possible they take up a brush and dip it into bright colours, ready to paint a bright picture out of a dark situation. They spend all day building flimsy walls around their fragile lives, to keep problems out. Then they cover them over with whitewash, passing fantasy off as reality. Exhausted by their life protection efforts they collapse in the midst of the construction of their fake world. In other words, they seek safety and security all the time. Deceiving rather than really believing.

I had a conversation with a concerned mother whose son was considering a mission venture into Afghanistan, one of the most dangerous places on earth at the time, and still is. Clearly concerned for her son's safety, she asked me how I would counsel her son regarding his desire to go. Regardless of what I wanted to say, and did say, the mother wanted me to place her son's safety and her having peace at night ahead of any desire by her son to sacrifice himself in service for God. The mother wanted me to agree with her and offer words of support and protection. I could not. The narrative that surrounded her belief was that God would want her son to consider family safety and security, including her ability to sleep well at night, before service and sacrifice. This is a common theme in the comfortable pews of the West, yet unheard of in the persecuted churches, where there is not even the luxury of pews. Is our life to be about security or service?

I have on occasion been privileged to serve in the training of pastors and leaders in places like Cambodia, Sudan, Uganda, Ethiopia and Kenya. As I prepare to go I invariably get asked, 'Is it safe where you are going?' or 'Aren't you concerned about your safety?' Or they ask my wife, Judy, normally in my presence, 'Are you worried about him going to such places?' Now I'm not saying that I have no safety concerns or that my wife does not share these same concerns. But what the inquirers are really saying is, 'Don't you think you should consider prioritizing your safety and security ahead of ministry?' My normal response now is to say, 'What response to your question should I give? Would you like me to reconsider and not go?' They then normally stutter and sheepishly say 'No, no, that is not what I am saying.' 'So what are you saying?' I then ask. They normally then fumble around and offer something like, 'Well I just think it would be good to consider if there are less dangerous places for you to serve God.' If we are honest isn't that what many of us are at times wanting and doing – serving God in the comfortable and safe places. We create comfort zones, zones so comfortable and so large that it would take a miracle for God to get us out of them. Ever wondered why there are more miracles outside our comfort zones than inside. Because you need them on the outside. On the inside you are too busy feathering your nest to even want a miracle. Security or service? Ministry means putting yourself personally on the line or going into circumstances and places where things are not under your control, where you actually, really need God. Ministry means sacrificing security for service.

Heart Fear

The heart fear of the whitewasher is crisis and disaster. They run a mile from anything that smells like trouble, from anything that could unsettle their safe trouble-free world. Quickly they build a flimsy artificial wall of safety around their lives and paint it white to make it look holy and good. What do you do when faced with problems and crises? Do you deny their existence? Do you frantically build and paint, pretending? Or, do you rest in the peace of God's love and power? What is your picture of God?

As a parent you take your first child to school. It's the first day. You are naturally uneasy, even fearful. Anything could happen to them you think silently to yourself. So you pray with a mixture of helplessness and desperation. 'God protect my child, please!' As you anxiously leave the classroom and walk out the school gate, what do you think? 'God has given me this child to protect so I must do all I can' or perhaps, 'There is no way God would want anything bad to happen to my child; He will care for them.' But as you make the journey home you are not completely at peace. You are not completely sure that you can rest and just trust God. After all you know of families, Christian families, who have lost children in unfortunate accidents. And so you turn the car around and start to build your own wall around the safety of your child.

Back at the school you sign up to be on the parent help roster as often as possible. An opportunity comes up to regularly help in the school canteen; you are there. You're not paranoid – the school needs your help, you justify. There is an opening in the library to help three days a week. Not only does the school need your help but it appears that God needs your help as well. It feels so much safer when you help God care for your child. You can now watch and care for your child almost every day of their school life. You feel so much more at peace when you are building walls of safety into your life. But then, the first child goes to high school and the second and third are still at primary school. What now? Stretch yourself to breaking point, watching and protecting? Or rest and trust?

If you have a heart of a whitewasher you don't want problems in ministry. You think this is God's work and He wants everything to go smoothly, professionally, and without a hitch. After all, you are serving God, and it's hard work, and He wouldn't want you to go through any more suffering, would He?

I remember one particular business meeting at a church where I was pastor. I had recently graduated from college and was the first pastor of the church. I had probably been working there for about six months, focusing on the pastoral care and the teaching and training aspects of the church. Being the first pastor of the church many people appreciated there being someone to talk to about anything and to help them deal with the many problems they faced. Marriage difficulties, issues with sexuality and addiction, parenting problems, and many more rose to the surface for the first time because someone was there to listen. Then in the middle of the business meeting, an unsolicited comment, completely out of context was dropped onto the table with a loud thud. 'Now that we have paid pastors in the church, we have more problems than we have ever had. I'm not sure that appointing a pastor was a good thing.' Their thinking, like many of us, is that church ministry should be about reducing problems; it certainly should not multiply them. I replied, 'Well if you want to invite sheep into the barn you need to put up with the manure on the floor.' In other words, 'If you invite sinners into the church don't be surprised if there's a mess.' As Jesus said, 'It is not the healthy who need a doctor, but the sick.'[7] Our heart fear of problems can so easily create walls around us that will close down and prevent the opportunities of ministry rather than open us up to all that He wants to do if we would just rest in Him. What is our picture of God in these situations? An eraser of problems or a healer of people?

Approaching the border of the Promised Land the people of Israel, searching for certainty like fire lighters, asked Moses to send some men ahead of them into the land to spy it out and bring back a report. So Moses sent twelve men off to spy out the land. Upon their return Moses asked them to give an account of what they saw in the land. Ten of the spies gave a bad report. Acting out of fear they reported that in comparison many in the land looked like giants, and they like grasshoppers.

---

7   Mark 2:17

Their fear led them to give a negative report, leading others into disobedience to God in order to fulfil their own selfish and cowardly agenda. They died of a plague and transmitted a plague of fear onto a generation who died wandering in the wilderness.[8] Fear stopped obedience.

The picture the ten spies had of God was small. How quickly it had shrunk. Not long ago their God was huge, delivering them from Pharaoh, dividing the sea, and defeating opposing nations as He brought them safely to the edge of the Promised Land. But now they are overcome with fear for their own safety. It seems their powerful God has diminished and is now unable to care, protect and deliver them. As Moses said:

> You saw how the LORD your God carried you, as a father carries his son, all the way you went until you reached this place. In spite of this you did not trust in the LORD your God, who went ahead of you on your journey... to show you the way you should go.[9]

The other two, Joshua and Caleb, were different. Their God had not shrunk. Perhaps, as they remembered all He had done in their minds and lives, He had grown. Now they were ready to place their lives in the hand of God and trust Him in any future challenge. They knew that while man may destroy the outside, fear kills the inside.

The son is imprisoned in Afghanistan, the child is badly injured on a school excursion that you did not attend and the people and problems in the church loom large. What then? What is your picture of God? What do you do? Bury you head

8   Numbers 13–14, Deuteronomy 1:19-46

9   Deuteronomy 1:31-33

in the sand in denial, hoping everything will go away? Renew your efforts to build walls of safety and security in your life that you know will eventually be found out to be fake and flimsy and will fall? Or rest in the faithfulness of God, knowing His purposes and perspective is beyond our own? As C. S. Lewis writes of Aslan the lion, representing God, 'he is not safe, but he is good.'[10]

The exiles in Ezekiel's time were called to turn and rest again in God and believe that even though it appeared that God had abandoned His home in the Promised Land, He had not abandoned the promises to His people. They need not be afraid, they need not look to false prophets and they need not build flimsy whitewashed lives. But would they rest in His arms? Will you?

Heart Demand

When we scrape the whitewash off the wall of our hearts what do we find? Strength and rest in God and His promises, no matter the circumstances? A heart that denies the problems, that lives in a false reality, a house with a whitewashed wall around it? Or a life that is frantically seeking to control circumstances to provide a facade of safety and security attempting to eradicate any possibility of disaster or crisis? What is our heart demand? Protect us from, or peace despite?

Our conversations can be very telling, revealing our real heart agenda. Bad news arrives from out of nowhere. Whether it is from the local news, a telephone call, a prayer point announced at church. What does your heart do? What are the thoughts that race through your mind? What is your heart

---

10   Lewis, *The Lion, the Witch and the Wardrobe*, 75.

demand? 'Don't unsettle my world!' 'Protect me!' Or 'Tell me everything is going to be OK!' So we gather others around us to see what they think about the news. We hope that they will tell us that everything will work out, there is no real crisis, or that it won't affect us. Certainly, that is what we are loudly telling others, trying to convince ourselves in the process, hoping they agree. We so easily deceive ourselves.

While the city builder prays for success, and the fire lighter prays for certainty for the way ahead, the whitewasher will use prayer as a security blanket against the dangers of the world. They will fervently request that above all God forms a protective shield around their life exempting them from any problem, crisis or tragedy. Take a look at your prayer list, or in the absence of a list, the dot points that form in your mind as you come to prayer. 'Please protect my children today.' 'Please keep us safe as we travel.' 'Please remove the problems in our workplace.' 'Please sort out the difficult people at church. And God why are there difficult people anyway?' 'Please make all the sick people better.' 'And just in case I forgot to mention it before, please protect our family from any disaster.' While we live in a broken world, we believe we should be able to escape the drama of life through the covering of prayer.

While these types of prayers aren't wrong in themselves, they tell us about what we expect of God; how we think life should work according to our own heart agendas and demands. We ask God for safety and comfort, to pander to our agenda, not for perseverance despite the problems, which may just be His agenda. The picture of God that we enjoy is one where God is always there to sort things out for us, where He never leaves us to just trust and have faith in Him despite the difficult circumstances that surround us. Those in exile had this same picture of God. God is there to make life comfortable and safe for us. If Ezekiel is telling us bad news, we will get someone else to tell us good news to cover up our anxiety. Our heart demands good news from God and others. We want to live in a fake reality, not the real world. We are happy with fake news, not reality and truth. We want to escape, and we think God should help us. And if He won't we will look for our own ways of escaping and finding the security we so eagerly desire.

It's so easy to treat relationships in this way, as an escape from reality and as a guarantee of security. Perhaps we have been struggling through life to feel safe, stable and secure. Then all of a sudden it seems possible; the right person comes onto the scene and offers the security of love. A big security boost! A wall against the crises and problems of life. We feel loved because we feel safe. But, did we fall in love prepared to care and even suffer for the other, no matter what difficulties or tragedies come our way? Or do we fall in love with the other because they protect us and provide a wall that feeds our heart's desire for peace and security? When our heart strongly demands security in the world, all relationships become something we use to build our walls of safety, rather than opportunities to express the love of God in its fullness. Our demands are so high, needing to receive so much from others, leaving very little time and energy to think about giving generously to others. We frantically grasp at others for our survival, rather than restfully loving them. Protect me or I will leave you becomes the basis of our relational investment. Then we get married and with our voice vow to be there for the other through thick and thin. All the while we anxiously hope that we will live happily ever after in a peaceful utopia, far, far away from trouble. Or at least having now married a security officer, surely they will protect us from the ups and downs of life, which deep down we know exist. Did we just marry, an act involving God, hoping that we have signed a life insurance policy, to protect us from an 'Act of God?'[11] So while we verbally promise sacrifice, our heart actually demands security, 'till death do us part'. We need to ensure our relational heart and vows do not look something like this:

> I need to feel safe and secure in your arms and I expect you to meet that need by protecting me in every situation; by avoiding conflict through agreeing with me at all times; and by constantly offering your strength to help build a wide and strong comfort zone around our lives. I want you to make me the most secure person in the world. My goal in marrying you is to find my security in you.[12]

Our heart agenda of safety and our heart demand for protection leads to an uneasy heart problem.

Heart Problem

Our problem is we can't rest. We can't rest in the hands of God in the midst of the storm. We are restless, anxious and fearful.

When someone is sick, we are restless. We want everything to return to normal and quickly. So what do we do? Because our life has been unsettled, we do whatever we think is best, not so much to make them feel better, but so we can feel better about ourselves. At least if we have done something, administered some medication, then the problem should get better we reason. In our restlessness we can be more concerned about our own heart problem than the other's medical condition. We can be

11 In insurance terms an 'Act of God' is an event considered to be an unexpected and unexplained disaster.

12 Crabb, *The Marriage Builder*, 31.

trying to solve our problem, to get rid of that which signifies to our heart that all is not right.

Just yesterday, before I sat down to write, I had a conversation with a young lady. 'Jesus and I are not going so well,' she offered. 'I know I should trust Him completely, but with all that has happened in my life I find it hard, and now I feel like I'm always expecting things to go wrong, and I blame God for it. I want Him to protect me and keep me safe, but I fear He won't. I have been abandoned so many times that now all I feel like doing is shutting my heart off and trying to protect myself from the pain that others cause, and that God allows, the best way I can.'

As whitewashers we often live life as victims. Rather than embracing life we respond to life's circumstances as victims, angry at God and others. We find we can't really trust God for good things. Or we receive good things in our life but are always waiting for bad things to happen. Then we rail against God saying, 'See, I can't really trust you; what good are you if you can't even protect me and make my life safe? I'll find something or someone else to cover and protect me.'

So we paint whitewash. We control our homes, we install security systems. We control our children's lives; we plan and track their weeks, days, hours, and minutes. We stalk their activities and whereabouts on our phone. We avoid risks and discourage others from taking them. We hate sermons that feature topics of sacrifice, perseverance, persecution and pain. We cover ourselves with stories of slayed giants, calmed seas, and closed mouths of lions. We do not dwell on the narratives of walking in fire, being beaten and stoned, or shipwrecks and snakebites. We plan the need to trust God out of our lives. Does that mean we are faithless? We certainly are not faith-full.

Sadly, we often desire to live in a fake reality, desiring not to be disturbed, even by God. But God desires that we live in this present reality with Him, attentive to His voice. John Lennox in his book *Where is God in a Coronavirus World?* puts it like this:

> In a fractured world, damaged through the consequences of human sin, pain and suffering are inevitable. Perhaps we had hidden from this reality until coronavirus rampaged across the globe. Now we cannot ignore it....

Lennox continues, first quoting C.S. Lewis:

> 'We can ignore even pleasure. But pain insists upon being attended to. God whispers to us in our pleasures, speaks in our conscience, but shouts in our pains: it is His megaphone to rouse a deaf world.'

> Perhaps the coronavirus might function as a huge loudspeaker, reminding us of the ultimate statistic: that one out of every one of us dies. If this induces us to look to the God we may have ignored for years, but who wore a crown of thorns in order to bring us back into relationship with himself and into a new, unfractured world beyond death, then the coronavirus, in spite of the havoc it has wreaked, will have served a very healthy purpose.[13]

Through all the drama, turmoil, problems, and disappointments of life, when nothing seems secure, God is calling us to rest in His safe arms. All the while our heart agenda says, 'I can't rest. I must keep whitewashing to try to cover over the problems and protect my ever-anxious heart.'

---

13   Lennox, *Where Is God in a Coronavirus World?*, 49.

God's Heart Agenda

God's agenda for our heart is that we rest in Him rather than being restless. He wants us to live at peace in the midst of life, despite all that surrounds us. He wants us to know that it is all in His hands. He wants those in exile to not try and build flimsy whitewashed security walls around themselves or to pretend that the world is OK when it clearly, because of the disaster of sin, including their own, is not.

God told Abram 'I will make you into a great nation and I will bless you...'[14] And this was what the exiles were holding onto. How could a God who said this then abandon His land, temple, and seemingly His promises, and allow this disaster to fall on them? They had forgotten God's words to their ancestors as they prepared to take possession of the land. Through Moses God said:

> If you do not carefully follow all the words of this law, which are written in this book, and do not revere this glorious and awesome name—the LORD your God... You who were as numerous as the stars in the sky will be left but few in number, because you did not obey the LORD your God. Just as it pleased the LORD to make you prosper and increase in number, so it will please him to ruin and destroy you. You will be uprooted from the land you are entering to possess. Then the LORD will scatter you among all nations, from one end of the earth to the other. There you will worship other gods—gods of wood and stone, which neither you nor your ancestors have known.[15]

This is a prophecy of their abandonment of God and of the ensuing judgement and destruction. Interesting, isn't it? God,

---

14   Genesis 12:2

15   Deuteronomy 28:58-64

in judging His people and sending them into exile, was being faithful to His earlier promises, given at the edge of the Promised Land. Now the exiles were demanding that God not carry out the words of Ezekiel and be unfaithful to His earlier promises. All to give them, one of the generations who were responsible for precipitating the judgement, a comfortable, peaceful and secure life. Idolatry and sin had brought judgement and disaster into their world. But God had not left them. According to the visions of Ezekiel, God had left His temple to go with His people into exile in Babylon. God was always with His people. What's more Ezekiel's words did not conclude there. His book ends with the promise of the restoration of the people and a restored city given the name, 'THE LORD IS THERE'[16] as if to underline again the fact that God never left them, so trust and rest in Him, no matter what.

Jesus Himself understood this idea of rest in the midst.

> Then he got into the boat and his disciples followed him. Suddenly a furious storm came up on the lake, so that the waves swept over the boat. But Jesus was sleeping. The disciples went and woke him, saying, 'Lord, save us! We're going to drown!' He replied, 'You of little faith, why are you so afraid?' Then he got up and rebuked the winds and the waves, and it was completely calm. The men were amazed and asked, 'What kind of man is this? Even the winds and the waves obey him!'[17]

Look at the contrast here. Jesus is in the boat in a storm, asleep. The disciples are in the boat in the same storm, afraid. They are so afraid for their lives they are calling out for salvation. What is the point of the story? It is not that Jesus will calm every storm of

---

16   Ezekiel 48:35

17   Matthew 8:23-27

your life, like the exiles were hoping, and like so many sermons we have heard that echo in our hearts. But it presents a contrast between a life of faith and a life of fear.

I don't think Jesus was surprised by the storm, do you? After all, He could create them. He came to visit this world, a world that He created; He knew what was here. It appears that Jesus was also not overly concerned by the storm. Hence the sleeping. Why? He knew whose hands held His life, and that His ultimate place was at the side of the Father. He knew nothing could change this. He was safe and secure in the midst of the storm, resting in the Father's hands.

What about the disciples? They feared for their immediate future. At this point in their journey they seemed to have no immediate or ultimate hope. And they either did not know or yet believe that with Jesus, who was held by the Father's hands, they were safe and secure, despite the raging storm and the threat of disaster all around. Seeing their fear Jesus connected it with their lack of faith. He knew they had no reason to fear, because He was with them. They didn't yet understand that they too could rest with Jesus, in the Father's hands.

This event should have served to focus the disciples' minds toward faith in Jesus, away from a consuming focus on the surroundings and circumstances. The same is true for the exiles. Abram was given a promise of a people and a land, under God. They had ended up in Egypt for 400 years, and yet, despite the circumstances, God, true to His Word, had rescued them and returned them as a people to the land. The exiles should have thought, 'Our God is a faithful God, He keeps His promises, He rescues us and He restores us. So we can rest in the hands of God, in the midst of the uncertainty and insecurity of Babylon.'

The same is true for us. Don't be surprised by the things that happen. We live in a broken, sinful world. Bad stuff happens. Not because God doesn't care; He came to show us how much He cared. Not because He is not strong enough; after all, He calmed the waves. But His agenda for our life is not our comfort or even our safety but to mature our faith and our relationship with Him, in the midst of life and all that surrounds us. He is not always about calming the storms of life. But He is always about building our faith in the midst, which should also calm our fears.

In His prayer to the Father just prior to His death Jesus says:

> My prayer is not that you take them out of the world but that you protect them from the evil one.[18]

His prayer for the disciples and for us is not for relief from the problems of the world, but for strength to stand in faith, not giving in to the devil, in the midst of the storms of life. What is our cry to God in the storm? 'God, take me out of here' or, 'God, please take this away.' Do we pray for relief only or for faith and strength to stand in the midst? Do we desire to escape and demand that God remove or change the circumstances, or are we content to just be held by God?

While Judas was doing his betrayal deal, Jesus was in the garden talking to His disciples. He talked to them about leaving, returning, telling them the way, and sending the Spirit, and then He said:

---

18   John 17:15

I have told you these things, so that in me you may have peace. In this world you will have trouble. But take heart! I have overcome the world.[19]

Really? You have overcome the world? At the exact same time you speak these words you are being betrayed and hunted down like a criminal to be charged, tried, convicted and crucified. Look, right now Judas is entering the garden with a detachment of soldiers who will take you away. Have you really overcome?

But Jesus knew who held His life. In other words, we should not be surprised by the circumstances, the coronavirus, or any present problem or disaster, any more than by any other trouble that has ventured upon this broken and decaying planet. It not only needs renewal but is looking forward to it. Any crisis is just another sign that we are not in heaven yet and that the world is groaning, awaiting its coming transformation.[20] Sin, disease and the curse have not won. We, along with this groaning world, are awaiting the final glorious transformation into newness.[21] We know that Christ has overcome all through His amazing loving sacrifice for us. We know that He is victorious over sin, death and the grave. We know that He will return and wipe every tear from our eyes, that there will be no more death, or mourning, or crying or pain. For the old will pass away and He will make everything new.[22]

It's like watching a football game for the second time. When you watch the game live you are anxious for your team – will they win, or won't they? You sit on the edge of your seat, heart

---

19   John 16:33

20   Romans 8:19-22

21   Romans 8:23

22   Revelation 21:4-5

pounding, nerves tingling, adrenaline flowing. But when you watch a replay of the match knowing they have already won, it's very different. While still excited, you are at rest; you can sit peacefully, enjoying the moment because you know exactly how it all works out, and you find yourself celebrating the victory even before the game ends. With God we know the end before it happens. He has overcome; we can now celebrate and rest in eager anticipation.

So we take heart, right now; in the midst of all this chaos, we take heart. We trust. We have faith. We rest. Do we? What is our response to the situations we find ourselves in? Faith or fear? Do we take heart, having faith, living in the certain knowledge that no matter what, God has us in His hands? Or do we live out of fear, relentlessly trying to keep control of our lives, looking for comfortable whitewashed answers, trying to create our own safe nests, believing that God has not overcome?

Simply put, what do we believe? Will the world overcome us? Do we operate out of fear and panic now that we have apparently lost control over our lives? Or, knowing that God has got everything firmly in His hands, and that whatever we are experiencing is nothing more than a sign of a groaning world awaiting its transformation, we throw ourselves into His arms, casting all our cares on Him?

We are not immune to the suffering, death and heartache that the world often brings us. But like Paul we can say:

> I consider that our present sufferings are not worth comparing with the glory that will be revealed in us.[23]

---

23   Romans 8:18

Denial, panic or peace? That's the choice. What is your response? Deny that the world is broken; paint everything a glossy white, pretending that all is OK with the world, hoping that no disaster strikes? Live in a frenzy, believing that if you are active enough and keep a step ahead of every conceivable problem, you will have the world around you under your control, and that the flimsy whitewashed wall should hold? Or choose peace, resting in the arms of Him who has overcome all?

We are in a storm. Will we rest in the one who can calm the storm? He may not stop the storm just now, but one day He will, on that final day. Can we hold on and live, in rest, in faith, in trust, and with perseverance run the race marked out for us?[24]

He wants us to rest and trust in Him despite all the problems and circumstances that surround us. He wants us to know that true life, life eternal, is being held by Him. And that it can overcome our fears and insecurities. 'I am with you always'[25] He says, 'rest in me.'[26]

---

24 Hebrews 12:1
25 Matthew 28:20
26 Matthew 11:28-29

Summary

Text & Focus: Ezekiel 13:10-11

> Because they lead my people astray, *saying,* 'Peace,' when there is no peace, and because, when a flimsy wall is built, *they cover it with whitewash*, therefore tell those who cover it with whitewash that it is going to fall.

Heart Agenda:	*Security*
Heart Fear:	*Crisis*
Heart Demand:	*'Tell me everything is OK!'*
	'Don't unsettle my world!'
	'Protect me!'
Heart Problem:	*Resting with God and others*

Reflection Questions

1. Is being a whitewasher a problem in your life?

2. In what areas of life do you look for security?

3. In what areas of life do you feel you want to deny reality?

4. In what life circumstances do you feel restless and try and control them by yourself?

5. When do you require others to protect you?

6. In what areas do you find it hard to have peace?

7. Do you struggle to really rest with God? Why?

Well Diggers

5

Well Diggers

The Story

At the time that God was commissioning the young prophet Jeremiah, the people were leaving God to worship other gods, and to worship even what their hands had made from wood and stone.[1] Jeremiah was a priest and a prophet, born around 650 B.C. He served as God's mouthpiece for around forty years, from the thirteenth year of the reign of Josiah, when he was around twenty-three, until the exile of the people of Judah to Babylon and the destruction of Jerusalem in 587 B.C. by Nebuchadnezzar. Jeremiah's prophecies provide the reason why God allowed Jerusalem and Judah to fall into the hands of the Babylonians – divine judgement![2]

---

1   Jeremiah 1:16
2   Jeremiah 4:11-12

In the early days, the people of Israel had been devoted to their God. They had left the abundance of Egypt, and with confidence in Yahweh had followed Him on a long unfamiliar journey. During this pilgrimage God had jealously protected His people, like a husband protects his bride. Enemies of the Israelites were destroyed as the people of God sought to honour Yahweh. What had changed? Why had the people strayed from God? Why had they started to follow worthless idols? Had they forgotten that God had miraculously led them through the barren wilderness and brought them safely into the fertile Promised Land?[3] Did they not learn from their recent history, when God had allowed the Assyrians to attack Samaria and their unfaithful relatives in the northern parts of Israel, taking them into exile in 722 B.C.? Apparently not. 'In spite of all this, her unfaithful sister Judah did not return to [God] with all her heart.'[4] They had forgotten all that God had done for them in the past; they had even forgotten God Himself, and gone looking for the good life elsewhere.

As a result, in Jeremiah 2:11-13, God, through His prophet, brings this charge against His people:

> 'Has a nation ever changed its gods? (Yet they are not gods at all.) But my people have exchanged their glorious God for worthless idols. Be appalled at this, you heavens, and shudder with great horror,' declares the LORD. 'My people have committed two sins: They have forsaken me, the spring of living water, and have dug their own cisterns, broken cisterns that cannot hold water.'

---

3   Jeremiah 2:3-8

4   Jeremiah 3:10

God calls the heavens to witness this charge. 'Look' He says, 'be appalled and shudder with great horror.' This is completely unexpected; has it ever happened before in the history of nations? Has a nation ever changed its gods? Never! is the implied answer. God must have thought, 'Why have my people, the people that I cared for so powerfully and so intimately, in rescuing them from Egypt, delivering them from their enemies, why have they now given up on me to follow other gods? Why would they give up on the glorious living God and go their own way to pursue *"The Useless Ones,"*[5] worthless idols made of wood and stone? It has never happened before; it makes absolutely no sense whatsoever. Why?'

The answer is in the image of the broken cistern. Cisterns in Israel, then and now, may be likened to wells or dams built on farms. They are constructed catchments designed to gather and store precious water. Israel is a land of low rainfall. The average annual rainfall for Jerusalem is only 66cm. Thus every landowner would prefer to have access to a creek or flowing spring on their land. Having a never-ending supply, rather than dig an unreliable and finite cistern out of the side of the hill is obviously preferable. But springs were in short supply in the land, so cisterns were commonplace. The cisterns were mostly hewn out of limestone rock and the inside was sealed with lime plaster to stop the life-giving water from escaping. The land of Israel is given to extreme variations in temperature and to earthquake tremors. Repairing the resulting cracks in cisterns was a laborious and repetitive task. Who would exchange the opportunity to have a farm with a continuous spring, for land

---

5   The term worthless idols in the Hebrew literally means 'the useless ones' or 'they that do not profit'. Thompson, *The Book of Jeremiah*, 170.

without one, needing a cistern that provided limited supply, which invariably leaked, and required constant repair?[6]

In other words, who would replace the living God who supplies eternal springs of living water, with idols, a cistern, the 'useless one'? Who would choose something that would break, could hold water for only a limited time, could not truly satisfy, and would ultimately end up empty, needing to be repaired and refilled time and time again?

God is stunned by their choice. In doing this the people of God have committed two sins. They have forsaken God and they have pursued worthless idols that cannot provide life-giving streams. Why drink from the streams of other gods? Why drink from the Nile in Egypt, or take your fill from the Euphrates in Assyria? Why seek life from the idols of these foreign lands?[7]

Indeed, why did these people give up on the living God and chase that which cannot satisfy? Why would they seek to find life among gods who were clearly dead? What was their heart agenda?

Heart Agenda

They didn't believe that God could give them the fulfilment they desired from life, so they began to create other cisterns searching for a life that would satisfy. They became well diggers. Their heart agenda was their own fulfilment. They were consumed with their own happiness. Sound familiar? This is true for so many of us today.

---

6   Bromiley, *The International Standard Bible Encyclopedia*, (V1):702. Dearman, *Jeremiah and Lamentations*, 59. Thompson, *The Book of Jeremiah*, 171.

7   Jeremiah 2:18

It seems as if the miracles, deliverances, protections and presence of God with them in the past had become like vapour in their minds. As if the events of Noah, Abraham, Joseph, Moses, Joshua, Gideon, David and Hezekiah had vanished from their history. It was as if the faithfulness of Yahweh in the past and the promises for the future provided less for life now than the immediate physical reality of the wooden and stone gods of the surrounding nations. In their minds the past and the future provide nothing immediate; only the present fulfils and satisfies now. So let's go dig a hole for ourselves and be satisfied. Who cares if it leaks? Let's get our fill now! After all everyone else around us is doing it.

Do we feel like this? Do we feel as if the actions of God in the past do not satisfy us now? Perhaps they feel like ancient sands of time that have slipped through our fingers, hard to hold onto, bringing no life to us now. And maybe we feel as if the promises of the future, even though they seem amazing, somehow are elusive, too distant to satisfy us. We feel they are like a shimmering desert mirage, off in the distance. They look great, but we fear that if we start to count on them too much, get too close, reach out to take hold of them, they will disappear into nothingness. No life there we feel. So we dig. We need something now. 'Fill me!' we cry.

What had they done? The text is clear; it says that they had exchanged their one God, and chased after many false gods. They had forsaken the one true permanent living stream, to drink from the many other temporary sources that they provided for themselves. Leaving the living God for lifeless idols, they abandoned true life for the mirage. Be appalled.

But we also do it all the time. We depart from God to go and dig our own wells. We search for other places of satisfaction apart from God. A desire to be satisfied is one thing but satisfying it apart from God is quite another. What we are doing is doubting that God is enough.

In the Garden of Eden everything was created good. Everything was created to worship God and for relationship with God. All was well until that moment – that moment of temptation. When Eve was tempted by the serpent God's goodness was called into question. The serpent said,

> Did God really say, 'You must not eat from any tree in the garden'?[8]

The serpent created the possibility of doubt in Eve's mind. 'Did God really say?' grew to, 'Why did God say?' to thinking, 'This fruit looks good; is God holding out on us?' to, 'Can God be trusted?' and, 'Is God good?' God's goodness was doubted and the path to self-fulfilment was created. Don't trust God for good things; trust yourself and be satisfied now. So Eve acted, took the fruit, and was filled. Sin came from doubting God's goodness and deciding to satisfy ourselves apart from God.

Our heart is so easily addicted to our need for fulfilment, to our desire for immediate gratification, our worship of self. Let's go back and take another look at the Israelites at the foot of Mount Sinai. Remember Moses had gone up the mountain for a time, forty days. The Israelites came through the Red Sea and into the desert following Moses to worship Yahweh. And now it seems that both have disappeared. While the fire lighters in search of certainty asked, 'Who will lead us now?' the well diggers cried out, 'Who will we worship; who will satisfy us now?'

---

8   Genesis 3:1

So Aaron took their gold and made a false god for them to worship. They worshipped and indulged themselves in revelry.[9] Because God and their leader were not there to provide them with the answers to their immediate desires and demands, they went looking elsewhere. They were not satisfied with the faithfulness, presence and provision of God in the past. Nor were they content with the promises of a new land in the future. They wanted more now. Their heart agenda for immediate satisfaction had led them, in the face of a momentary feeling of lack, to quickly replace the God of all life, with a god of all lies.

This desire for self-gratification, for immediate satisfaction is an addiction to self-worship, which is then expressed in a myriad of ways, all designed to achieve a feeling of fulfilment, relieving that horrible feeling of emptiness. So we end up like the Israelites in the desert, or facing exile in Jeremiah's time, digging our own wells of satisfaction, worshipping our own idols of addictive relief and gratification.

Heart Fear

Our heart agenda for fulfilment comes from the fact that we are desperately afraid of feeling empty. Indeed we are not designed to be empty or feel empty. We are created and designed for the fullness of relationship with God and others. We are designed for perfection. But our doubting in God, our selfish path of rebellion, our choice of self-worship and self-fulfilment over trusting in the goodness of God, has left us in a broken and cursed world, outside of Eden. We are unsatisfied, unfulfilled, empty, and we hate it.

---

9   Exodus 32:6

Just like the Israelites who felt abandoned in the desert we are disappointed with the brokenness of the world because we are designed for perfection and perfect relationships. We want Eden, or heaven. Now! But it's not here. We want everything to be perfect now. But it's not. We want no problems, no pain, no crisis, no virus and no worries. We want our own significant, certain, secure and comfortable life here on earth. We want our best life now. Heaven is coming. But it's delayed. We feel abandoned. We feel as if God has let us down, and so off we go to dig our own wells, searching for our own shallow places of life, hoping they will satisfy, because we feel so empty.

So if we can't have heaven now and we can't wait for heaven, what happens? We find we are living with an ache. We have a nagging sense of disappointment with the world, an insatiable longing for more. What do we do? We are tempted to try anything to either satisfy our longing for more or to escape the emptiness and pain of life. So we go and dig our wells of self-satisfaction. We dig our leaky cisterns of sex or success, of sports or shopping, of Facebook or fashion, of TV or travel, of drugs or pornography, of adoration or alcohol, of gaming or gambling, of Instagram or ice cream, of chocolate or the cinema, of food or parties, of leisure or any other pleasure. And more, more, more, now, now, now, until we are a slave to our unquenchable desire to relieve the feeling of emptiness and replace it with some form of gratification, no matter how superficial or fleeting. Until we find ourselves addicted to a cycle of self-satisfaction, of self-worship, of self-fulfilment.

Let's take a closer look at this addictive cycle of emptiness and fulfilment. Try and feel it inside yourself as we go. Living in this sinful and broken world you say to yourself:

1. I long for more; I feel empty
2. I deserve to feel satisfied, to be full
3. I will seek satisfaction or relief
4. I find satisfaction or relief in ...
5. I feel good ... temporarily
6. Now, if I'm honest, I'm empty again

So now you feel bad, empty again. The well has run dry, the cistern is broken, and now you long even more to feel good, to find satisfaction. And around and around you go. Let's reflect on those uncertain, not sure, empty, sort of 'yuk' moments in life. Where do you go? What do you do to relieve the emptiness and find fulfilment? Do you go to God or false gods? To the living water or to dig your own well?

While I was studying at Bible College, I developed a very spiritual fulfilment addiction, which I must admit still reappears occasionally. I would get to that emptiness moment; that 'yuk', unsure, stuck in a boring assignment, sick of revising for an exam moment. Then at that moment I would feel the longing for something more. After all, I have been working so hard, I deserve to feel satisfied and full, not bored and hollow. Some people might have gone to the fridge for a drink or for ice cream. Others to the pantry for chips or chocolate. Others would turn on the TV. Still others may have gone shopping or called a friend to go out for coffee. Others would have gone nowhere, just flicked to another screen to become lost in online information and images. But I would get in my car and find myself driving to the local Christian bookshop, about a 15-minute drive, quick and easy to get to. And I would search through all the theological books, the Bible commentaries, the church and pastoral ministry books for anything new or exciting and, if possible, on sale. I would always buy something. After all, it was on special, it was an investment in my studies, and I don't drink or smoke, so this is OK – it's Christian. During the course of my studies I found myself regularly going through this book buying cycle thinking nothing of it. And you, like me, may not think this is a problem at all, especially in comparison to all the other possible cycles of relief and fulfilment. At some level that is true, but it is not taking my longing and emptiness to God first. It is trying to provide myself with my own source of satisfaction. I am well digging. Yes, the well may appear small and harmless. Nevertheless it is my own well of fulfilment designed to relieve my momentary feeling of emptiness. And of course it doesn't satisfy, so that's why I return again and again to the same well and now have a library the size of a rather significant cistern. Book buying is not wrong; filling your emptiness moments with something other than God is.

You do this too. Every time you say I deserve an evening out, or some pampering, or new clothes, or a holiday, or even just a piece of cake, you are saying I feel something is missing, I am less than full, I need a refill, another hit of satisfaction. So you look for a way to relieve the emptiness and to obtain the desired object or experience. For a time you get a buzz, you are satisfied on some level, but the excitement fades, the novelty wears off, the drug runs out, the cistern leaks, and the well runs dry. But you are afraid of emptiness so off you go again, in search of another dose. You know deep down it doesn't work; it doesn't last. But you go chasing after fulfilment again, at first in the same broken well, or you try something new, something bigger and better, something that comes with more promise. But alas, that also fails you.

We can also use people as substitute wells. Do you know someone who is a social sponge? A social sponge is someone who sucks the life out of people. When they enter the room you never quite know what to expect. Sure there is always drama and excitement, never a dull moment. But it always seems so intense and it requires a lot of you. It seems like you have been sucked into the vortex that is their life and you are not sure when or where you will be spat out. At the end when they leave, you sigh a big sigh and you fall in a heap, exhausted. Not only did you get sucked up into their whirlwind life, but they have also sucked the life out of you, and then left. They have gone. They were fun to be with for a time. You gave them everything, but they gave you nothing in return. They took as much life out of you as they could and when you became exhausted, they left, and moved on to sap the energy and life out of another. You probably gave an inadvertent or maybe blatant sign or sigh, communicating that you had had enough, you had lost energy or interest, and you were done. You had nothing more to give. And they were not satisfied; their well was still leaking, so they continued to dig elsewhere. They long for more. They feel empty again. They tell themselves they deserve to feel satisfied, fulfilled. So off they go, to another conversation, another party, another relationship, in search of satisfaction or relief. They extract the life out of another moment, another person, another situation, seeking to temporarily relieve their feeling of emptiness. They feel energized again, but it ends and they feel flat again, empty. Around and around they go, always seeking more yet never satisfied. Like an eternal sponge. To you they seem full of life, like everything is rosy, like they are the epitome of the abundant life, yet inside they feel empty, and no amount of engagement or excitement seems to satisfy. Another day, another well, another broken cistern, empty.

This is like the situation of the woman who Jesus went out of His way to meet in Samaria. She was found at noon at Jacob's well, needing water. Not only was her bucket empty but her life was also. As Jesus, thirsty Himself, sat down, His focus was more on the well digging that she was doing in her life rather than the drawing from the well that she needed to do each day. Jesus saw past the obvious – she's out of water – and reached toward the hidden – she is relationally empty, searching for fulfilment from broken cisterns. The woman had had five husbands, and now she was living with another man who was not her husband. She was trying to find her fullness, not in God the living water, but in relationships that kept on breaking and leaving her empty. She, like the Israelites, thought that life could be found apart from God, and so she, like they, left God in search of other gods, or in her case other men.

When Jesus found the woman, she was empty. She was digging through the lives of others trying to find that everlasting stream that would continue to satisfy. The woman had a bucket, but was empty; Jesus had no bucket, but was full. Jesus looked into the well, and seeing a picture of what He saw in her life He said:

> Everyone who drinks this water will be thirsty again, but whoever drinks the water I give them will never thirst. Indeed, the water I give them will become in them a spring of water welling up to eternal life.[10]

Upon hearing this the woman said,

---

10   John 4:13-14

Sir, give me this water so that I won't get thirsty and have to keep coming here to draw water.[11]

Her fear of emptiness drove her from one relationship to the other seeking to satisfy the demand of her heart. Empty again she hoped Jesus would satisfy that demand. She would try anything at this point.

Heart Demand

When I was growing up, getting a job was more about finding security and significance. I chose to follow the accountancy and business field. Nowadays it seems that it's all about satisfaction and fulfilment. People start things and stop things. Unsatisfied, they pursue a new direction; they change courses and jobs like coffee brands searching for the most pleasing option. They want an easy path into a cool career that offers them everything they desire. And why not? Everything we desire now, please, sounds like a great life. But maybe it also sounds just like a child noisily demanding an ice cream from their parents.

Our well-digging heart expresses itself most clearly through two childlike demands that we often constantly make of life and of others. 'Make me feel good!' and 'Satisfy me now!' 'Get me that ice cream,' we demand, 'and now!' Let's put this into a ministry and a relational context.

After struggling to fit study into your busy and satisfying social life you graduate from Bible College or seminary and are finally ready for your first pastoral assignment. Leading a church is all you have ever dreamed about since you were young. It's a dream about to come true. You have prepared for this for so long. You have imagined the first sermon, the church

---

11   John 4:15

response, the pleased look on the faces of the hearers. You have imagined the satisfaction of being in the precise place that you believe God intended for you. Now at your first service as pastor, you move forward to take the pulpit as the congregation sings the final line of the final song. The microphone is on, the PowerPoint slide is in place, and you look out into the eyes of the expectant congregation. What are you thinking? 'This will make me feel good, finally!'

You have been a lead singer in church for many years now. Singing has been a big part of your life. You started as a young teenager. An older musician heard your voice and suggested you come and try out for the singing team. You were good – the people loved you, they accepted you, and perhaps for the first time you felt affirmed. You continued and the people repeatedly praised you. Every time you performed you felt that sense of satisfaction. You began to live for those moments. Those brief moments in the spotlight where you were praised and made to feel full. But they faded. It seemed like each time you performed you needed more light, more applause, more affirming comments to feel satisfied and fulfilled. And you noticed how empty you began to feel midweek as normal life crowded out the experience of the weekend. Somehow serving the church through singing now seemed more of a chore than a delight. The weekly satisfaction slowly disappeared and only a lingering emptiness remained.

But fortunately you were spotted by the leader of a well-known megachurch who was looking for a new lead singer for their music team. Their team not only perform for large crowds, multiple times a week, they also put on concerts, and create and record their own music, releasing their own albums. They are a household name across the country, at least in Christian circles.

You took the position, changed churches, joined the team, began practising, and it was your first big night. You take to the stage, dazzled by all the lights, and you head over to your microphone stand. What are you thinking? 'I will be satisfied now!'

Whether we are like the Samaritan woman chasing fulfilment in a new relationship, or like the social butterfly seeking life in the next casual encounter, or like the pastor chasing praise from the congregation, or like the singer seeking the satisfaction of the spotlight, the heart demand is the same. Make me feel good now! This is true whether we express this demand in the pursuit of career advancement, in the purchase of increasingly flash cars, through the next extreme adventure, or just in the acquisition of the next dress, fantasy novel or box of chocolates. They are all the same: a search for fulfilment and satisfaction in all the wrong places. They will all provide the same result, emptiness, and a cycle of searching for more and more and more.

The irony is that that which seems very present, very now, very real, and very fulfilling, is actually not compared with God who we think is not present, not now, not real, and not fulfilling, but who actually is. Yet we continue as if we don't seem to care. We are bent on trying to feel good now, to find heaven here, through other gods.

But we are not in heaven yet. Yes, we have the spring of living water in Jesus, but this life, here and now, disappoints. If we seek to be completely satisfied here and now, through digging wells anywhere other than in our relationship with God, they will leak, and eventually dry up. Yes, heaven is coming. But we must learn what it means to long for a heaven that is not yet here, at the same time to be dissatisfied with this broken world, and yet also be satisfied that we can find all we need in God, not in our range of alternative broken cisterns. If we don't, our heart demands will lead us only to empty, dry places, and eventually to some form of breakdown or burnout. Burnout is an absence of life due to unfulfilled expectations. Your heart is empty. Your fear has become your reality.

Heart Problem

When you are empty or burnt out, what can you give to others? What sustaining life or meaningful service can you offer? Nothing. When you are in this state your focus is on how you feel and where you are going to find some form of life, rather than how you can give sacrificially of your life to God or to others. At this desolate place survival rather than service becomes the priority.

If we find ourselves here, we should not beat ourselves up, as if we are the only ones who have come to the end of ourselves. Even the great prophet Elijah suffered from this form of despair. Alongside all of the miracles that God performed through him, Elijah had just participated in one of the most spectacular. God had showed up to defeat the 850 prophets of Baal and Asherah in an amazing display of power, bringing a decisive victory. He should have been on top of the world; God was obviously mighty, all powerful, and on his side. Yet when Jezebel, the wife of King Ahab, heard what had happened she threatened to kill Elijah. So, what did the mighty man of God do?

> Elijah was afraid and ran for his life. When he came to Beersheba in Judah, he left his servant there, while he himself went a day's journey into the wilderness. He came to a broom bush, sat down under it and prayed that he might die. 'I have had enough, LORD,' he said. 'Take my life; I am no better than

my ancestors.' Then he lay down under the bush and fell asleep.[12]

If we take our eyes off God, the source of all power and life, we quickly sink, become empty, and are ready to give up. We find ourselves no longer in a place to serve God and others, as we have nothing to give. And because we feel so empty, we are no longer sure God is good. So rather than focusing on God for life we feel the overwhelming urge to take it from other places so that we feel good now. We become takers not givers.

God's Heart Agenda

Sara comes from Cambodia, and James from South Sudan, two of the most war-torn and poverty-stricken countries on earth. They are both very good friends of mine, and both pastors of their people. In a conversation over mediocre coffee in a café in Siem Reap during the annual pastors' conference in Cambodia, James says to Sara,

> You know what the best part of our life is? We started out in life with absolutely nothing. You were discarded by your family and had to beg to survive. I was born in the bush under a tree with nothing, no food, no clothes and no education. Both of my parents died when I was young, and I was treated like a slave by my uncle who raised me. We were both considered by the people of the world to be rubbish. We had nothing when we found Jesus. When we found Jesus, we then had everything. We experienced the absolute joy of knowing Him in our nothingness. And now God has blessed us with other things, but it is only the joy of knowing God that sustains us. The richer people, on the other hand, they have so much

---

12   1 Kings 19:3-5a

already when they find Christ. And they often just add Christ into all they have. Many never really experience only having the joy of Christ. They have so many things in life to sustain them already.

Perhaps that is the problem. Those of us with much have confused the abundant life with Christ, with the good life here plus a dash of Jesus sprinkled around now and then. The Israelites had done similar. They had gone pursuing the good life by chasing other false gods, all the while effectively leaving the living God back in the temple, relegated to hosting a festival now and then. They were not finding true life, full life, all of life in God.[13] They seemed satisfied with broken cisterns and empty wells. Are we? God wants so much more for us. Just like with the Samaritan woman, He wants us filled with living water that never runs dry.

Job had everything and it was getting up the nose of Satan. Satan thought that Job only worshipped God because he was so blessed. He thought that God had put a hedge around his life and protected his prosperity and this was the sole cause of Job's ongoing faithfulness to God.

If we are not careful, we can find that we have the same mind as Satan. Thinking that having blessings here and now is evidence of God's favour and the reason one would worship God in return. And that if everything goes south, we are justified in cursing God. The thinking goes like this: you get from God, life is good, the good life I have here is the abundant life God has promised and is the reason we would worship God in return.

But Job proves this to be completely wrong. God allows Satan to take everything away from him except for his very life.

13   John 10:10

Satan took away his sheep, his oxen, his camels, his servants, even his sons and daughters. Satan, like Job's wife, must have thought that Job at this point would abandon God and give up on Him as a source of life and the one to worship. But he was wrong; in the face of such pain and suffering Job said,

> The LORD gave and the LORD has taken away;
> may the name of the LORD be praised.[14]

What would you have done – gone searching for a better god elsewhere? Obviously, life for Job wasn't tied up in the things of this world. Even the loss of his family didn't tempt him to curse God and die. So what was he holding onto as a reason to continue to praise God? 'It must be his health' Satan thought. Upon request God granted Satan the right to affect Job's health. The next picture we see is Job in constant pain, sitting among the ashes, scraping the sores that covered his body. It's time to give up on God, his wife maintains. 'Curse God and die!' she says. But Job would not give up on God's goodness and His faithfulness despite the tragic circumstances of life. Despite the possibility of any satisfaction and fulfilment coming from the good life here and now having vanished, Job drank from a deeper source saying,

> Shall we accept good from God, and not trouble?[15]

For Job, God alone was his life, his source of everything.

The story of Job continues with late-night debates and long discussions with his friends. God must have thought, 'Will they never run out of their futile ideas and words?' So God turns up.

---

14   Job 1:21
15   Job 2:10

Breaking His silence He gives Job and his friends a front row seat to His grand panorama of life, the universe and everything show. God reveals to Job who really has life in His hands. Job sees his place, our place, in the grand order of things, confirming that life is not about us, it is about the God of all life. It is only in God that we find any real life, satisfaction and fulfilment.

But will we believe it? If we are just adding God into our already full life, meaning our life is full of stuff from this world, and are busy digging our own wells, the answer will be no. Our desire for fulfilment and our fear of emptiness will distract us and tempt us to dig other wells and cisterns, seeking life elsewhere first and God last. And we will wind up cracked, broken and empty. However, if like Job, Sara and James, Christ is everything because we have nothing else as a source of alternative life and satisfaction, total satisfaction and fulfilment will be found in relationship with Christ.

James, in his New Testament letter to the scattered Jewish Christians, echoes the words of Jeremiah to those seeking fulfilment apart from God when he says,

> What causes fights and quarrels among you? Don't they come from your desires that battle within you? You desire but do not have, so you kill. You covet but you cannot get what you want, so you quarrel and fight. You do not have because you do not ask God.[16]

Jeremiah knew, James knew, and the Samaritan woman found out. All other paths, all other wells, do not satisfy. No matter how many you try, no matter how many you dig, they are all broken and eventually run dry. You do not have fulfilment because you do not ask God.

---

16   James 4:1-2

SUMMARY

Text & Focus: Jeremiah 2:13

> 'My people have committed two sins: They have forsaken me, the spring of living water, and have *dug their own cisterns*, broken cisterns that cannot hold water.'

Heart Agenda:	*Fulfilment*
Heart Fear:	*Emptiness*
Heart Demand:	*'Make me feel good!'*
	'Satisfy me now!'
	'Relieve me please!'
Heart Problem:	*Giving to God and others*

REFLECTION QUESTIONS

1. Is being a well digger a problem in your life?

2. In what areas of life do you look for fulfilment?

3. In what situations do you find yourself feeling unsatisfied and empty?

4. In what ways do you demand that others make you feel good?

5. In what life circumstances do you feel like you need to find some relief? How do you find it?

6. Why is God not enough for you in these empty times?

7. Do you struggle to give to others and God? Why?

Foot Washers

6

Foot Washers

We have lifted the lid on our heart and uncovered the hidden agendas that reside sometimes deep within. To point us in a new direction we return again to Jesus and Peter and the other disciples in the upper room.

Jesus knew His hour had come to die. If ever there was a place of no significance, no certainty, no security, and no fulfilment, it should have been with Jesus, facing imminent betrayal, an unfair trial, and the prospect of being put to death by the most cruel method ever devised, crucifixion. Yes, Jesus felt the awful prospect of what lay ahead. We will soon see His sweat falling like great drops of blood as He agonizes in the garden. But here in the upper room prepared for the Passover, Jesus saw the world through different eyes.

Peter and the other disciples entered the room and took their place around the table. Finally Jesus arrived, and as He had the habit of doing, He turned the whole room, actually the whole world, upside down, again.

> Jesus knew that the Father had put all things under his power, and that he had come from God and was returning to God; so he got up from the meal, took off his outer clothing, and wrapped a towel around his waist. After that, he poured water into a basin and began to wash his disciples' feet, drying them with the towel that was wrapped around him. He came to Simon Peter, who said to him, 'Lord, are you going to wash my feet?' Jesus replied, 'You do not realize now what I am doing, but later you will understand.' 'No,' said Peter, 'you shall never wash my feet.'[1]

Peter struggled in Jesus' world – it was all upside down to him. Jesus constantly talked with sinners and tax collectors. He even ate in their homes. He touched lepers and sat down at a well for a chat with an outcast Samaritan woman. You had to deny yourself and take up your cross. The first had to be last. If you followed Him, you had to be a servant of all. The powerful were to serve the weak and vulnerable. Even the children were important in the kingdom of God. What a world! And now as if all that wasn't enough, Jesus wanted to wash their feet like a slave. 'Where is the servant who is supposed to do this? We can't just let Jesus become like a nobody,' Peter must have thought. It was hard for him to let go, to put his sword away, to stop trying to make the world fit into his agenda and let Jesus show him that it's OK to live in an upside down world, because from the perspective of the one who holds it, it's always right side up. It's also hard for us to let go and view things from a point outside

---

1   John 13:3-8

ourselves, where we are not the centre of everything, and to see things through Jesus' eyes.

Jesus loved the disciples to the end, completely. He knew He was leaving them soon. He knew they would struggle to deal with His upcoming death. He knew this would shrink their sense of significance. Who wants to be associated with a dead Messiah? He knew this would shake their sense of certainty. What would they do without the one they had followed for so long? He knew it would upset the sense of safety they had grown to enjoy at His side. Where would they find comfort in a world that was hostile toward them? He also knew that compared to the last few years, they may suddenly feel empty and unfulfilled. Where would they find their purpose and satisfaction now? Perhaps they would be tempted to go and chase it in other places. Maybe they would try fishing again. So He decided to show them how to really live.

Jesus, knowing the end was near, loving His disciples completely, wrapped a towel around His waist, poured water into a basin, and prepared to do the task reserved for the lowest person around: to wash the disciples' feet. Why was it so easy for the creator of the world to take on such a lowly role? A role that not even the Jewish slaves carried out, but that was commonly reserved for the gentile slaves.[2]

Firstly, He was significant. Jesus knew who He was. Throughout His time on earth we see the Father break open the heavens on several occasions and shout to His Son, 'This is my Son....'[3] Obviously for Jesus there was never any doubt about who He was and whether He was significant in His Father's

---

2   Burge, *John*, 369.

3   Matthew 3:17, 17:5

eyes or not. Jesus knew He was the very loved Son of God. His identity was connected to being the Son of God.

Secondly, He was certain. Jesus knew. He knew where He had come from and where He was headed. No doubt. He had come from God and was returning to that same place and position. He knew that nothing could change who He was, that He belonged to the Father, and that His future was always with Him.

Thirdly, He was secure. God had put everything under His feet. He had been given the ultimate position of power. That is as secure as it gets. He knew that this power could ultimately defeat death and bring about the resurrection. That is why He could say to Martha after Lazarus had died, 'I am the resurrection and the life.'[4]

Finally, He was fulfilled. The voice from heaven didn't stop with, 'This is my Son ...' it continued saying, '... whom I love, with him I am well pleased.'[5]

What amazing confirmation. What amazing satisfaction it must have brought Jesus to hear His Father exclaiming this from heaven. Jesus was both loved by the Father and affirmed for being completely obedient to the Father. Jesus found His fulfilment, His purpose, in the midst of the lavish love of God and in the joy of serving Him. Hence His extraordinary love for the disciples and His willingness to serve them so sacrificially, so completely, to the end, to the point of dying for them, for us.

Jesus didn't have any hidden agendas fighting to restrain Him from taking on such a humble position of love and service. All of the agenda items were taken care of by the Father. Knowing who He was He got up to serve. He wrapped the towel around

---

4   John 11:25

5   Matthew 3:17, 17:5

Himself and carried the basin over toward Peter. Placing it beside Peter's feet, Jesus reached out His hand to wash the dirty, dusty, smelly, unclean feet of the fisherman.

But Peter abruptly put a stop to the whole operation. 'No!'[6] he said. 'This is not the way the world works. Jesus you deserve so much more than this,' he must have thought. 'It's all upside down.'

What is this 'much more' that Peter thought Jesus deserved? Whatever it was, how could Jesus be given more than He already had with His Father? Our hidden agendas are always pushing us, prodding us to desire more, and more, and more. More significance, more certainty, more security, more and more fulfilment. We, like Peter, would be tempted to say to Jesus 'Don't do it. Don't you realize what a spectacle you are making of yourself? You deserve to be so much more than a slave.'

Jesus could see the tremendous confusion swirling around in Peter's mind, so He leaned over and said,

> You do not realize now what I am doing, but later you will understand.[7]

What I hear Him whispering to Peter is, 'You think I deserve more. What you don't understand now is that I already have it all. When I rise from the dead, then you will understand that everything is significant, certain, secure and fulfilling, in the hands of the Father. What is more, the will of the Father is that I completely give my life for you so you can have it all as well.'

Jesus served them by washing their feet, showing His complete love for them. Then He gave them a meal, the bread

---

6   John 13:8

7   John 13:7

and the cup, to remember Him by. To remember how He loved them and how the creator of the world had carefully taken their feet into His hands. How He had wiped each foot that He had hand crafted, cleaning them, welcoming them to the family meal. To remember how He had loved them to the end; how the very next day He had died for them, was buried and rose again. To remember that He had their lives in His resurrected, cross-marked, eternal hands. To remember that He is now waiting to welcome them to recline around the heavenly table and share in the ultimate wedding feast.[8]

Isn't it true that like Jesus we already have the same position in the hands of the Father? Isn't it true that we, because of Jesus' gift of life to us, are now sons and daughters of God, brothers and sisters of Jesus, having complete significance in His eyes?[9] It's also true that we, like Jesus, have a certain future. Just like He knew He was returning to the side of the Father, we also know for certain that we have a special position as the bride of Christ, at the Father's table, and that He is right now creating a new home for us to be with Him where He is.[10] And isn't it also true that the same power that raised Jesus from the dead and secured His position, secures our position and our eternal inheritance? This power is far above any other rule, authority, power and dominion, leaving us safe in His arms. [11] And that nothing can separate us from the love of God?[12] What more can we want? We are totally safe and secure. Again, just like Jesus could bathe

---

8   Luke 12:35-40, Revelation 19:6-9

9   Romans 8:14-17

10   John 14:1-4

11   2 Corinthians 4:15, Ephesians 1:19-20

12   Romans 8:37-39

in the overflowing and abundant love of God, completely fulfilled, so it is with us. The apostle John puts it like this:

> See what great love the Father has lavished on us, that we should be called children of God! And that is what we are! ... Dear friends, now we are children of God, and what we will be has not yet been made known. But we know that when Christ appears, we shall be like him, for we shall see him as he is.[13]

We are significant, certain, secure, fulfilled, like Christ, in the hands of the Father. No need to be tied up with hidden agendas. We can leave them behind and find everything in Christ. Yes, we agree with the text above that we don't experience the fullness of this yet and long for so much more. But as we wait for this 'more', which is certainly coming, we also realize that we cannot find this 'more' in anything this broken world has to offer. Babel is now rubble, our torches blow out, our flimsy walls fall down, and our broken wells run dry. So we focus everything on the one who is our all in all, our tower of significance, our light of certainty, our secure fortress and our fulfilling living stream.

Jesus places the basin and towel back at the side of the room and reclines with His disciples at the table once more. He says,

> Now that you know these things, you will be blessed if you do them.[14]

We are called like Peter and the disciples to put aside our hidden agendas so that we can serve and love God and others to the end, just as Jesus was able to serve and love to the end. Jesus knew who He was, so He could serve and love His Father and others completely.

---

13   1 John 3:1-2

14   John 13:17

Peter had followed Jesus before but that was a mixture of following and of hoping everything turned out like he planned, according to his hidden agenda. Peter's first encounter with Jesus by the Sea of Galilee changed his life. I don't think it was the abundance of fish that affected him the most; it was the realization that he was sinful, and yet Jesus had bothered to bless him with abundance and invite him to be one of His disciples. He was made to feel significant, certain, secure and fulfilled within His band of followers. Peter began to slowly build a new life around following the Messiah. He mixed his own agenda items into his life with Jesus. At first, he found his life had renewed purpose with Jesus, but slowly it seems he built a life of purpose around his newfound position of significance and importance and the possibility of real power at the centre of Jesus' messianic mission.

But that moment was a distant memory. It had quickly faded with the taking and killing of his leader. The world had fallen in on him and he had returned to his old world of fishing. It took one final lakeside encounter for Peter to truly understand and lay down his agendas. Jesus again meets Peter beside the Sea of Galilee. He asks Peter whether he loves Him more than his own life, which includes his own agendas. The tension is real, and Peter struggles to respond. Jesus has to ask him three times, letting the gravity of the moment sink in. Will he lay down his life and love Jesus? Finally Peter says 'Yes!' Jesus says, 'Feed my sheep.' In other words, Jesus was telling Peter that true life comes from loving and serving God and others. Peter finally got it.[15] Then Jesus says to Peter one more time 'Follow me!' Peter does follow; this time, free of his hidden agendas, he loves and serves

---

15   John 21

completely, even to the point of dying as a martyr in the service of the gospel.

Saul was on the way to Damascus following a life filled with his own agendas. But he was arrested by the light of Jesus, was transformed, and lived a new life where his significance, certainty, security and fulfilment all came from his Lord and Saviour. He came to understand life, not separate from, but in Christ this way:

> For he chose us in him before the creation of the world to be holy and blameless in his sight. In love he predestined us for *adoption to sonship* (significant) through Jesus Christ, in accordance with his pleasure and will.... And you also were *included in Christ* (security) when you heard the message of truth, the gospel of your salvation. When you believed, you were *marked in him with a seal,* (certainty) the promised Holy Spirit, who is a deposit *guaranteeing our inheritance* (fulfilment) until the redemption of those who are God's possession—to the praise of his glory.[16]

In the upside down, right side up world of Jesus, He washed the disciples' feet, loving and serving to the end of life. Peter finally got there, loving and serving his Lord and others to the end of his life. So did Paul. What about you? Are you a foot washer? Are you prepared to lay down your idea of how the world should work, revolving around you, serving your sense of significance, or certainty, or security, or fulfilment, or any combination of each? Are you prepared to own your hidden agendas and to exchange them for a life where you draw all you need from the fullness of life with God, so that you can freely and fully love and serve God and others, to the end of life?

---

16   Ephesians 1:4-5, 13-14, (emphasis mine).

Summary

Text & Focus: John 13:3-5

> Jesus knew that the Father had put all things under his power,
> and that he had come from God and was returning to God;
> so he got up from the meal, took off his outer clothing, and
> wrapped a towel around his waist. After that, he poured water
> into a basin and *began to wash his disciples' feet,* drying them
> with the towel that was wrapped around him.

Heart Agenda: *Loving Service*

Reflection Questions

1. What do you find difficult in the upside down world of
    Jesus?

2. Where do you doubt being significant, certain, secure and
    fulfilled in the hands of God?

3. When do you, like Peter, return to the familiar aspects of
    your life in order to avoid the fears of failure, uncertainty,
    crisis and emptiness?

4. Which hidden agendas are you most likely to be affected
    by?

5. Now that you understand your hidden agendas, what will
    you do when they appear?

6. Do you love God more than everything else?

7. What do you need to do now to love and serve God and
    others without hidden agendas?

Heart
Pilgrimage

7

Heart Pilgrimage

Having taken the time to consider the hidden agendas that often tie us up in knots and hinder us from effectively loving God and others, it's time to take a reading of our heart.

When I have presented these hidden agendas at conferences, in classes, as sermons or in conversations over coffee, I find that often for the first time people are able to actively monitor the pulse of their heart in these areas. So now it's your turn. What do you do?

You are walking toward the hospital, not a place you normally like to be in, and you rarely have cause to visit. But your friend has a complicated illness, and the diagnosis, treatment and prognosis are uncertain. Your mind is swirling with random thoughts. You enter the building, ask for direction, and finally find the right floor and corridor. As you enter the room your mind tries to find the right thing to say or do? You awkwardly go over and greet your friend. What do you think and feel in that moment? Is your focus on the other or on yourself? If it is on yourself, and you are a city builder, fearing failure you may think, 'I hope I don't embarrass myself with what I say. I need to make it significant'. The fire lighter in you might ask 'Is this the right thing to say or do?' and think, 'I hate moments of uncertainty like this'. The whitewasher inside you will scramble to find something positive to focus on, talking about life in general and the lovely flowers in the room. Ignoring the main topic you finally exclaim, 'Here I brought you a gift. I hope it helps you take your mind off things'. And as a well digger, if you turn up at all, you may feel good about yourself, fulfilled for the moment because you have done a good deed for the day. So let me ask you clearly and directly:

1. Are you a city builder? Are you pursuing significance, afraid of failure, striving to make a name for yourself, struggling to value God and others?

2. Are you a fire lighter? Are you chasing certainty, afraid of confusion, lighting your own fires, unable to trust God and others?

3. Are you a whitewasher? Are you seeking security and safety at every turn, afraid of any problem or crisis, frantically trying to make everything appear OK, unable to rest with God or others?

4. Are you a well digger? Are you constantly desiring fulfilment, never satisfied, afraid of emptiness, digging your own wells, trying everything, unable to give of yourself to God and others?

If you scratch below the surface and are honest you will find a little bit of every agenda hidden inside your heart. If you dig a little further, you will find that one or two areas preoccupy your thinking and are the stronger agendas that take you away from loving God and others to your full potential. For men it is often significance and certainty, fearing becoming a failure and being seen to be out of control in the eyes of others. So you do all you can to hold on to your name and provide a clear path. For women it is often safety and certainty, fearing a life that is unpredictable and out of control. So you do all you can, you hold on with all your might, and try and show to those around that you have everything under control. And for all of us there is that constant desire for fulfilment and our nagging fear of emptiness to deal with. So we hold on to our shallow leaky life, pretending that we are full, when in fact we are down to the last drop. Can we let go of our hidden agendas and fully trust and rest in the goodness of God?

These hidden agendas are like ropes that we allow Satan to use to tie us up, to stop us from really loving God, from really loving others, and from giving in sacrificial service to the end, like Jesus did. They bind us to selfishness, to a life of taking from God and others to serve self. They stop us from trusting God and others, from valuing God and others, from resting with God and others, and from a true giving of ourselves to God and others. Our desires, our hidden agendas, have bound us to ourselves. We need freeing.

The final thing that is released before a ship sails are the ropes that tie it to the wharf. Perhaps our ropes are these hidden agendas, the ropes of significance, certainty, security and fulfilment. After all, being at the wharf is significant. People can come and see us tied up at the harbour. They can marvel at the engineering and exclaim over the grandeur and the sheer size of the vessel. They can't so easily do that when we are out at sea carrying out our mission. When we disappear over the horizon, we are unseen. Better to keep the significance rope tied.

The wharf is so certain. There are infinite resources and supplies close by; we won't run out of anything. There are emergency and maintenance crews on standby; everything is planned and known. Not like when you are at sea. Who knows when a hurricane or storm, or fog, or an instrument failure may occur? Nothing out there is certain. If things don't work properly you could lose your way, or be left floundering in the open sea; better to keep the certainty rope tied.

At the wharf side we are secure. No hurricane or storm will affect us there. Even an onboard fire can be dealt with much more effectively. Emergency sickness can be treated immediately. We have all we need to keep us comfortable and to avoid problems of any kind. There are no icebergs or Bermuda Triangles here to destroy us or swallow us up: no danger, just peace. Why leave the safe haven of the sheltered harbour and go out there? Why risk it and untie the security rope? It's not safe and secure out there. We realize that we have got it all right here. We have the best of both worlds. We have the luxury, novelty and entertainment options aboard the cruise ship, and, if we want, we can go ashore to explore all the wonders and attractions that the region has to offer. We are fulfilled. Why go to sea, where your options are limited, where the feelings of nausea, isolation and boredom may grow, and the excitement and options of life may dwindle? Let's keep the fulfilment rope firmly tied.

Without knowing it our hidden agendas have tied us to the world in which we live and not allowed us to go to sea with God at the helm. But you say, 'I am a Christian. God is at the helm. He has control of my life. And what's more I am constantly asking

Him to reveal His will for my life. I'm ready to serve. But I'm yet to hear from Him.'

Well, His first word to you is 'untie'. Let go of the hidden agendas and allow Him to be your significance, your certainty, your security and your complete fulfilment. Yes, He will meet these needs through other people and circumstances at times, but they will always let you down. Untie yourself from the hidden agendas and start to move for God. You see God can only steer moving ships. If the captain of a ship moves the rudder from side to side on a stationary ship it only makes a small splash or a few ripples in the water below. Yes, maybe God is at the helm of your life, but if you are not untied from the wharf and have not started really moving for Him, how can He direct your life? If you are committed to attending to the hidden agendas in your life, then movement for God will be severely affected.

So you decide to untie. You take off the ropes of significance, of certainty, of security and of fulfilment, releasing the fears of failure, of confusion, of crisis and of emptiness, into the hands of God. And now you are free. Free of the hidden agendas, ready to sail, to truly love and serve God and others. You let go of controlling yourself and start to move with and for God.

'But where are we going?' you think to yourself as the land slowly fades from view. You quickly run to the bow of the ship to get a good view of the destination. We always want to know the end from the beginning. You look across two giant ropes neatly coiled near the bow. All you can see is sea and sky, a few birds and the line that marks the far horizon. Nothing; no clue. Any sign of significance, certainty, security, fulfilment? Not really. 'Where are we going?' you ask again. Then you hear a voice from the control bridge. It's the captain. He says, 'Don't look out the front, over the bow, go to the back and take a look from the

143

stern.' Confused you turn and slowly walk the length of the ship. Desperate for something, anything, you arrive at the stern and with anticipation look out over two more tightly coiled ropes that were just untied from the wharf. You blink; nothing. You get your binoculars out, still nothing. You look left and right, a few birds. You look down and you see the splash of the wake caused by the forward motion of the engines. Then again you hear the voice which asks, 'What do you see now?' Still confused you reply, 'Well, nothing really, just a few birds and the wake of the ship back to the far horizon.' 'And what does that tell you?' the voice asks. 'I'm not sure.' You pause and add, 'It shows where we've been, I guess.' 'Exactly!' the captain says. 'Looking back shows you two things. Firstly, it shows you where you have been and the various movements of the rudder that I have made to bring you to this exact spot now. Secondly, looking back, allows you to draw confidence for the future. In other words, if I have brought you this far, you can have faith that I will take you to the destination, even though it is beyond the horizon.' You stop and think for a moment, and say, 'So you mean that by looking back I can have faith to look forward with hope.' 'You've got it!' he says. 'Enjoy the journey.'

You then stand for hours at the stern of the ship, tracing the rudder movements of God in your life. Yes, there were moments of doubt and uncertainty. Yes, there were storms and crisis points. Yes, there were moments of feeling empty and insignificant. But those times were mostly when you were looking from the front of the ship trying to work out where your life was going all by yourself. But now, looking back, you realize that His hand had never left you; it had been gently guiding you all along. His faithfulness had brought you this far. You realize that while you could not see the destination, it was secure and certain in God's hands, and that it would be more significant and fulfilling than you could ever imagine. Now having heard God's voice, you trust Him and not the ropes for everything. Knowing you are His child and knowing His will is for you to faithfully love and serve God and others, you trust fully in His guiding hand and His faithfulness, not trying to satisfy your own hidden agendas.

God is moving the rudder. Are you making a small splash, tied up by your hidden agendas, or moving freely on a pilgrimage with Him? As the psalmist says,

> Blessed are those whose strength is in you, whose hearts are set on pilgrimage.[1]

Perhaps we could take the liberty to say it this way:

> Blessed are those who are free of their hidden agendas, whose significance, certainty, security and fulfilment is found in you alone, whose hearts are set on pilgrimage to love and serve God and others.

---

1   Psalm 84:5

Bibliography

Bromiley, Geoffrey William, ed. *The International Standard Bible Encyclopedia*, vol. vi. Grand Rapids, MI: Eerdmans, 1979.

Burge, Gary M. *John*. NIV Application Commentary. Grand Rapids, MI: Zondervan, 2000.

Crabb, Lawrence J. *The Marriage Builder: A Blueprint for Couples and Counsellors*. Homebush West: ANZEA, 1990.

Dearman, J. Andrew. *Jeremiah and Lamentations*. NIV Application Commentary. Grand Rapids, MI: Zondervan, 2002.

LaSor, William Sanford, and David Allan Hubbard. *Old Testament Survey: The Message, Form, and Background of the Old Testament*. 2nd ed. Grand Rapids, MI: Eerdmans, 1996.

Lennox, John. *Where Is God in a Coronavirus World?* Epsom: The Good Book Company, 2020.

Lewis, C. S. *The Lion, the Witch and the Wardrobe.* London: Lions, 1980.

Motyer, Alec. *The Prophecy of Isaiah.* Leicester: IVP Academic, 1993.

Oswalt, John N. *The Book of Isaiah Chapters 40-66.* Grand Rapids, MI: Eerdmans, 1998.

Thompson, John Arthur. *The Book of Jeremiah.* The New International Commentary on the Old Testament. Grand Rapids, MI: Eerdmans, 1980.

Also available from Christian Focus Publications...

The
TRUSTWORTHINESS
of GOD'S WORDS

*Why the Reliability of Every Word
from God Matters*

*Deeply biblical and thoroughly pastoral, this
book is a must-read for every Christian.*
– Scott Aniol

LAYTON TALBERT

The Trustworthiness of God's Words

Why the Reliability of Every Word from God Matters

Layton Talbert

This is a book about God's jealousy for His integrity, His passion to be believed, on the basis of His words alone. Throughout Scripture God expresses His determination to be known as the God who keeps His words. Learning to trust a God who is sovereign and in control, especially in the ache and throb of life, means hanging on to the conviction that everything He says is utterly dependable.

What does trusting God's words look like in real life and how has it played out in the experience of God's people? Let Talbert show you how in tracing the reliability of God through history we can learn to trust in with the future.

Layton Talbert demonstrates from God's own words that God is passionate about vindicating the complete integrity and trustworthiness of his words. All of God's words are reliable. God always keeps his words.

Andy Naselli

Associate Professor of New Testament and Systematic Theology, Bethlehem College and Seminary, Minneapolis, Minnesota

978-1-5271-0790-8

God's Spirit
The Antidote to Chaos

Reuben Hunter

God's Spirit

An Antidote to Chaos

Reuben Hunter

If we want lives that are marked by love, joy and peace, if we want to see goodness planted in the soil of our marriages and families, we need something we can't drum up from inside ourselves.

This book is a reminder and a profound encouragement for the Christian. You have been given the Holy Spirit through faith in Jesus Christ and He is working these beautiful qualities in you. You have the resources you need to live a life of love, joy, peace, patience, kindness, goodness, faithfulness, gentleness, and self-control. God has gifted this to you through His Son, so look to Him to grow and develop them in you; they cannot be found anywhere else.

We live in a chaotic and disorienting world, but Christians are not left without hope and help. God's Spirit: The Antidote to Chaos *shows us that the Holy Spirit is at work in the lives of his people, causing us to bear unlikely fruit despite the obstacles we encounter in our flesh and in the world around us. I found it to an enormously helpful and encouraging book – thoughtful, biblical, practical, hopeful, accessible, and wise. It is an ideal resource for those looking to grow in godliness.*

Mike McKinley
Pastor, Sterling Park Baptist Church, Sterling Park, Virginia

978-1-5271-0839-4

THE BIG TEN
Critical Questions Answered

SERIES EDITORS
James N. Anderson and Greg Welty

If Christianity is so Good, Why are Christians so Bad?

Mark Coppenger

If Christianity is So Good, Why are Christians So Bad?

MARK COPPENGER

It is reasonable to expect that the followers of Jesus Christ would exude the same sort of moral goodness that he did. But what does it mean to be good? What does it mean for the reality of the Christian faith that Christians fail to live up to the standards set by the Bible? Mark Coppenger engages with these questions.

The Big Ten: Critical Questions Answered is a Christian apologetics series which addresses ten commonly asked questions about God, the Bible, and Christianity. Each book, while easy to read, is challenging and thought–provoking, dealing with subjects ranging from hell to science. A good read whatever your present opinions.

This book doesn't whitewash the bad behaviour of many Christians, but it also offers some helpful insights, theological context, and practical wisdom for how Christians can respond to this important challenge.

Sean McDowell

Professor of Christian Apologetics, Biola University, La Mirada, California

Best–selling author and popular speaker

978-1-5271-0774-8

CONSPIRACY THEORY

When God is
Seemingly
Against Us

RICHARD GIBBONS

Conspiracy Theory

When God is Seemingly Against Us

RICHARD GIBBONS

If you have ever struggled with deep disappointments, unanswered prayers, or found your life crumbling around you, Conspiracy Theory was written just for you!

The world of social media shows us with real clarity the desire that people have to be connected to each other, but with the safety of an off switch. Real world intimacy can be very different – much better, but without the off switch. The greatest intimacy however is with God, whether we realise it or not. It can be difficult to take in the fact that God knows us better than we know ourselves, and that his love is bigger than anything we have ever experienced, yet not out of reach. The roadmap for this book travels through one of the most loved and popular portions in the Bible – Psalm 139.

With warm and wise reflections on one of the greatest songs ever written, coupled with engaging examples from across scripture, Dr Gibbons applies key truths about God's character and purposes in ways which are profound yet personal, and challenging yet life–changing, showing us how much God knows, cares, acts and loves.

Jonathan Lamb

Minister-at-large for Keswick Ministries, IFES Vice President, and former Director, Langham Preaching

978-1-5271-0726-7

BIG
HEARTED

*Are You Giving Happily
or Hesitantly?*

JOEL MORRIS

Big Hearted

Are You Giving Happily or Hesitantly?

Joel Morris

Every Christian is called to give – of our money, our time, our talents – but how often do we give just because we feel we should? We resent the sacrifice of things we could enjoy ourselves, and the biblical idea of giving cheerfully seems almost impossible. Or we give because we know that it will make us feel good. Or because we want other people to think well of us. But this is not godly giving.

In this concise book, Joel Morris explains that our understanding and practice of generosity is based on our knowledge of God, as well as the condition of our own hearts. While many books explain that we should give, Morris dives into the why of giving.

If we really believed that it is more blessed to give than to receive (Acts 20:35), we would not ask, 'How much do I have to give?' but, 'How much can I give?' In this much–needed book, Joel Morris shows us that a generous heart is the happiest heart, for it aims to imitate and glorify God.

Joel R. Beeke
President, Puritan Reformed Theological Seminary, Grand Rapids, Michigan

978-1-5271-0698-7

Christian Focus Publications

Our mission statement –

STAYING FAITHFUL

In dependence upon God we seek to impact the world through literature faithful to His infallible Word, the Bible. Our aim is to ensure that the Lord Jesus Christ is presented as the only hope to obtain forgiveness of sin, live a useful life and look forward to heaven with Him.

Our Books are published in four imprints:

CHRISTIAN
FOCUS
popular works including biographies, commentaries, basic doctrine and Christian living.

CHRISTIAN
HERITAGE
books representing some of the best material from the rich heritage of the church.

MENTOR
books written at a level suitable for Bible College and seminary students, pastors, and other serious readers. The imprint includes commentaries, doctrinal studies, examination of current issues and church history.

CF4•K
children's books for quality Bible teaching and for all age groups: Sunday school curriculum, puzzle and activity books; personal and family devotional titles, biographies and inspirational stories – Because you are never too young to know Jesus!

Christian Focus Publications Ltd,
Geanies House, Fearn, Ross-shire,
IV20 1TW, Scotland, United Kingdom.
www.christianfocus.com